HEALTH CANADA SERIES

DECISIONS FOR HEALTH

GENERAL EDITOR: Alan Robertson

Alan Robertson
Gordon Mutter
Jean Sanders
Ronald Wakelin

NELSON CANADA LIMITED

Published in Canada in 1981 by Nelson Canada Limited, 1120 Birchmount Rd., Scarborough, Ontario M1K 5G4.

Library of Congress Number 81-51398

Canadian Cataloguing in Publication Data

Robertson, Alan, 1936-
Decisions for health
For use in secondary schools.
ISBN 0-17-601751-8

1. Health education (Secondary). I. Title.
RA440.R62 613'.07'12 C81-094575-4

DESIGN: Artplus /Brant Cowie
COVER ILLUSTRATION: Peter Grau
TYPESETTING: Trigraph Inc.
PRINTING AND BINDING: The Bryant Press Limited

Printed and bound in Canada

81 82 83 84 85 86 87 88 89 90 91 11 10 9 8 7 6 5 4 3 2 1

PREFACE

Decisions for Health is part of a Canadian health program written especially for students in the intermediate grades. Because you are beginning to take more responsibility for yourself, it is important for you to learn ways to maintain your health and fitness and to understand the physical and emotional changes you are experiencing. You need to know what the right decisions for health are.

Decisions for Health is divided into two main parts. Part One looks at physical fitness and Part Two, at growth from adolescence to adulthood. To make this information easy to understand, we have included many of the most important ideas in photographs or cartoons. Examples and stories that help to explain the text are printed in coloured blocks beside it. Questions and activities at the end of each chapter will help you to recall the information and encourage you to explore further.

We think that you will enjoy learning about yourself as you read *Decisions for Health* and that you will find some answers to the questions you may have as you become an adult. We also hope that reading this book will persuade you to develop habits that will lead to a lifetime of health and happiness.

THE AUTHORS

The authors thank the following for their valuable advice on the preparation of this text: Anne Barrett, Consultant on Sexuality, Toronto; Warren Campbell, Co-ordinator, Physical and Health Education, Scarborough Board of Education; Dr. Anne Claessons, Hospital for Sick Children, Toronto; Audrey Dutton, Area Consultant, Metro Toronto Separate School Board; Dr. David Elliott, Wellesley Hospital, Toronto; Arline Gorelle, Co-ordinator of Physical and Health Education, Peel Board of Education; Douglas Harris, teacher of physical and health education, Scarborough Board of Education; Jennifer Hood, teacher of physical and health education, Etobicoke Board of Education; Charlotte Lackie, teacher of physical and health education, Etobicoke Board of Education; Douglas MacLennan, The Fitness Institute, Willowdale; Margaret Metzger, Nutritionist, Ontario Heart Foundation; Sharon Murphy, former Consultant, Physical and Health Education, Hamilton Board of Education; Dr. Ralph Persad, Ontario Ministry of Health; Norma Pickering, Kingston, Ontario; Jane Proctor, Clinical Supervisor, Physiotherapy Department, Scarborough General Hospital; Margaret Sheppard, Senior Research Assistant, Addiction Research Foundation of Ontario; Bob Simmons, Consultant, Values and Health Education, Etobicoke Board of Education; Joe Strobel, Consultant, Physical and Health Education, Scarborough Board of Education.

METRIC UNITS USED IN THIS BOOK

Symbol	Unit Names	Used to Measure
cm	centimetre	length or distance
g	gram	mass
kg	kilogram	mass
kJ	kilojoule	energy or work
km	kilometre	length or distance
km/h	kilometre per hour	speed
kPa	kilopascal	pressure
L	litre	liquid volume
m	metre	length or distance
mg	milligram	mass
mL	millilitre	liquid volume
mm	millimetre	length or distance

Units of time are not SI units but conform to SI style in this book:

h	hour	time
min	minute	time
s	second	time

TABLE OF CONTENTS

UNIT I
Physical Fitness and You

CHAPTER ONE
Introduction to Physical Fitness

CHAPTER TWO
Your Cardiorespiratory Fitness

CHAPTER THREE
You and Your Active Life

CHAPTER FOUR
Food and What It Does for You

UNIT II
How You Grow and Why

CHAPTER FIVE
The Beginning of Life

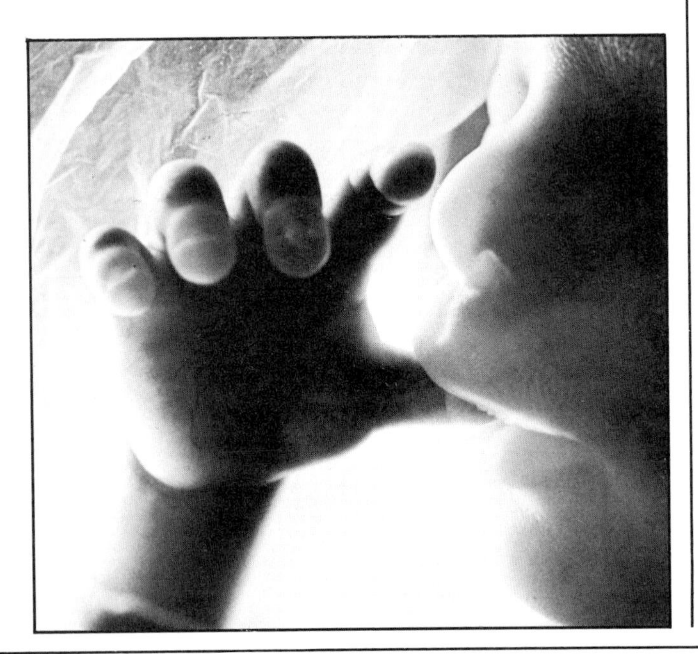

CHAPTER SIX
Your Adolescent Years

CHAPTER SEVEN
A Serious Health Problem

UNIT ONE

PHYSICAL FITNESS AND YOU

CHAPTER ONE

INTRODUCTION TO PHYSICAL FITNESS

WHAT IS PHYSICAL FITNESS?

Physical fitness affects your entire life. When you are fit, you look good, have lots of energy, and can cope with most of life's pressures. Even if you feel fit now, it is important to stay that way. A regular fitness program designed to meet your interests and abilities will keep you healthy and help you to work more effectively. You will feel positive about yourself and find it easier to be more productive and to enjoy an active life.

People who exercise have firm muscles and good body tone. Exercise will improve your circulation and help you to keep your mass at a reasonable level. By starting a program of physical activity now, you will also be contributing to your future health and appearance.

If you wake up in the morning feeling over-tired and unenthusiastic, you know you are not going to do well in school that day. Ask yourself if you are getting enough exercise. People who exercise often feel better and more alert.

Some days everything seems to go wrong for you and even a small incident can be upsetting. Some of the stress teen-agers feel is caused by hormonal changes in the body and by rapid growth. Your desire for independence or the pressures on you to accept new responsibilities may also cause tension. Whatever the cause, stress can lead to mental and physical problems.

Note: Words in boldface appear in the glossary of this book.

A FITNESS CHALLENGE

Maria, a grade nine student, joined the Outers' Club. The first outing was to be a hike up Blue Mountain. For those who made it, the instructor promised rock climbing the next month. Maria was not in good shape. She knew she would have trouble on the steep part of Blue Mountain but she wanted to do well so that she could go rock climbing. There were only three weeks before the hike.

Make a list of what Maria could do to upgrade her fitness for the hike up Blue Mountain. When you finish this chapter, check back to see if you would change any of your suggestions.

Knowing how to reduce stress is very important. One of the best ways to relax is to exercise. Even a 15 min walk will stretch tense muscles, improve your circulation, and release trapped energy.

You may think of yourself as physically fit because you hardly ever get sick, or because you can work and play hard without becoming overtired. However, being physically fit means more than this.

Physical fitness is the ability of the entire body (the heart, blood vessels, lungs, and muscles) to function efficiently with a minimum of effort. It can be divided into two general areas: fitness related to the actual health of your body and fitness related to your ability to perform certain physical skills. Each of these areas can be broken down into the following parts:

BODY HEALTH	PHYSICAL SKILLS
cardiorespiratory fitness	*agility*
muscular strength	*speed and reaction time*
muscular endurance	*power*
flexibility	*co-ordination*
ideal body fat	*balance*

A person who is physically fit, then, has not only a healthy body but a number of physical skills as well.

Certain physical characteristics are inherited, but you can always learn to overcome certain weaknesses or improve in some areas. It is much easier to increase your physical fitness if you know what you should work on and can plan activities that suit your own needs.

Body Health

This section will look at the five parts of physical fitness related to body health and suggest ways to improve them.

1. Cardiorespiratory Fitness

Cardiorespiratory fitness is the healthy functioning of the circulatory and respiratory systems. Fitness of the heart, lungs, and blood vessels is important in all strenuous activity that involves rapid intake of oxygen. Running and swimming are good tests of this fitness. If you can continue these activities for a long period of time without getting overtired and out-of-breath, your cardiorespiratory system is in healthy condition.

The **circulatory** and **respiratory systems** are central to all of your body's functions. Body cells need food and oxygen, and their waste products must be removed. The heart and lungs work together to circulate a new supply of oxygen-rich blood and to remove wastes such as carbon dioxide.

The heart is a muscle that can be strengthened. The lungs can be developed to greater capacity through exercise. Whether you want to participate in sports or simply enjoy an active and varied life, an exercise program to strengthen these vital parts of your body will benefit you.

Cardiorespiratory fitness is such an essential part of general fitness that it will be discussed in detail in Chapter 2. Tests for rating your own level of fitness are described on pages 46 to 49. Cardiorespiratory fitness is worth working for. You will feel so much better, you will be glad you made the effort!

2. Muscular Strength

Another important part of fitness is muscular strength, the amount of energy that a muscle can put forth. If muscles are used regularly, they become stronger; if not, they lose their tone and become weak. Muscular strength is important in maintaining vigorous activity and in delaying the onset of fatigue.

Though some people believe that strength development will make women muscle-bound and unattractive, there is no scientific evidence to prove this. In fact, strength exercises (even exercises using moderate weights) produce trim, well-contoured muscles in both men and women.

There are two basic types of exercise to develop muscular strength: **isometric** and **isotonic**. Isometric exercises are those in which the muscle is contracted but does not change in length. This is done by pressing or pulling against an immovable object or another part of your body. Some examples of isometric exercises are curls with a rope, wall push, and hand push.

Isometric Exercises

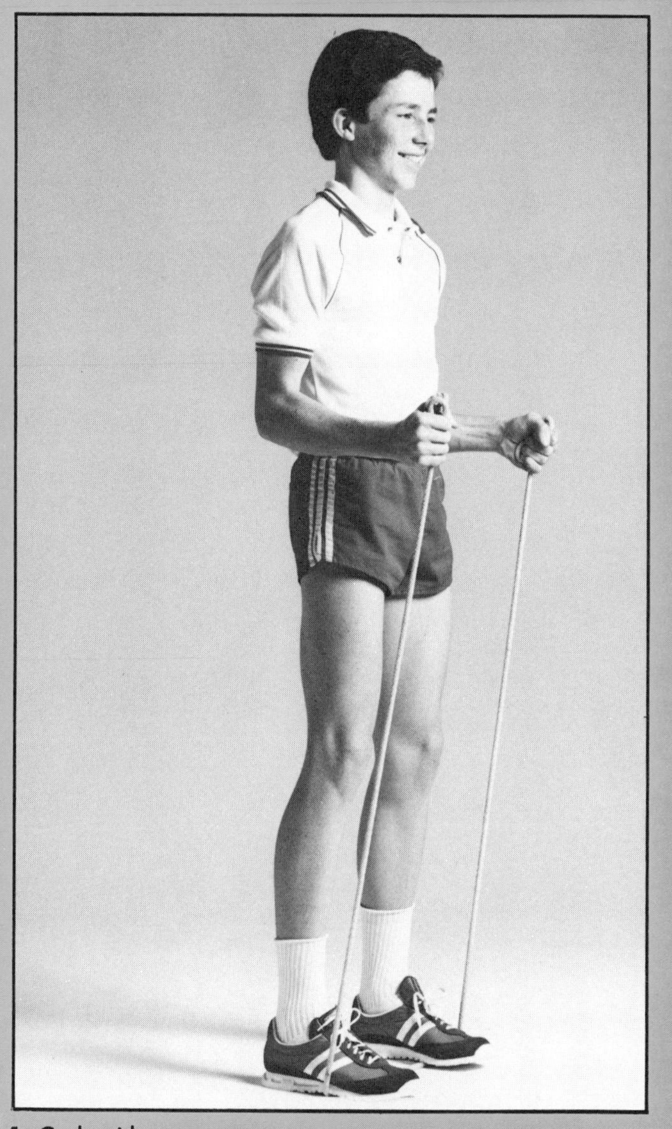

1. Curls with rope

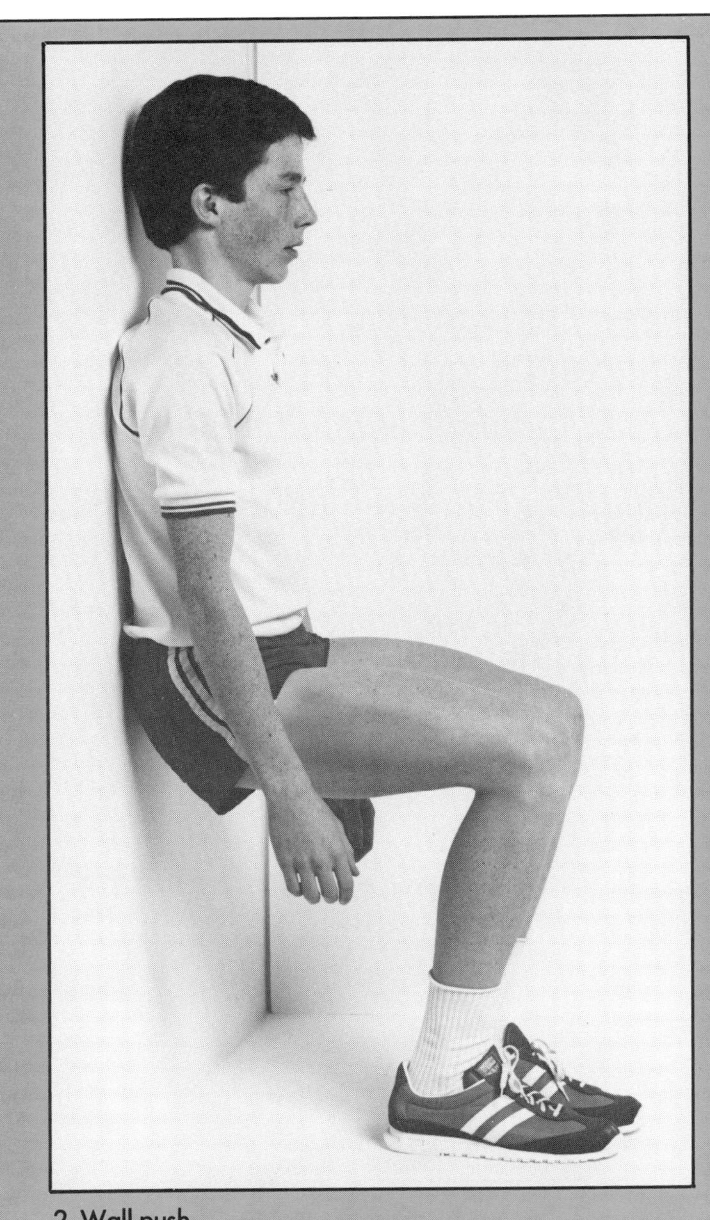
2. Wall push

3. Hand push

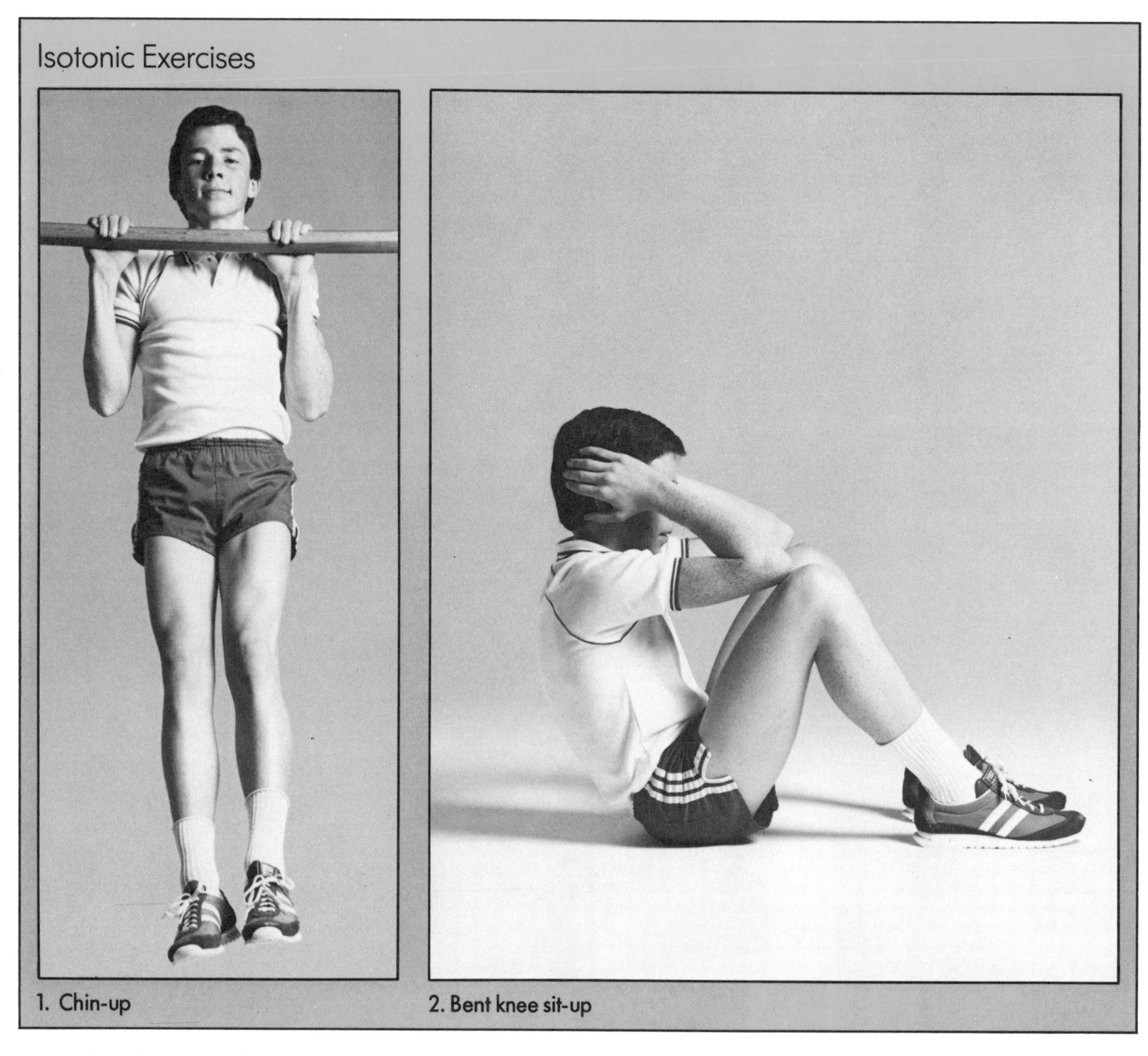

1. Chin-up

2. Bent knee sit-up

Isotonic exercises are those in which muscles are contracted or lengthened while working against a "load" or force. They are used more extensively in programs to develop muscular strength. A typical isotonic exercise is lifting a weight such as a barbell. Other isotonic exercises use the body as the load. Good examples of these are chin-ups, push-ups, and bent knee sit-ups.

Weight Training is a program of isotonic exercises using weights as the load to increase the amount of work the muscles must do. Some people confuse weight lifting with weight training. Weight lifting is a competitive sport in which an attempt is made to lift the greatest amount of weight in a specific manner just once. Weight training is an activity in which a specific load is lifted a number of times in succession for muscular development.

A program of weight training consists of a variety of exercises that involve the major muscle groups in the body, and generally requires three sessions a week. Each exercise should be repeated a certain number of times with a specific weight. Your maximum load is when you can lift a weight ten times with some effort. You should do all the exercises at one session. When each of these exercises can be done at one time without strain, you should increase the load or the number of repetitions during the next session. It generally takes from 4 to 6 weeks to improve your muscular strength through weight training.

Safety is important in weight training. Discuss your program with your instructor and check your weight load carefully before you start. You can easily be injured if you use a weight that is too heavy, or if you increase the number of repetitions before you are ready. It is especially important to be careful if you have not completed your growth, since you may more easily damage your joints. If you have to change weights on a bar, be sure that the collars holding the weights on the bar are firmly in place. When picking up the bar, keep your head up and your back straight. Then, lift by straightening the legs, not bending the back. Be sure to breathe while lifting the weight. Holding your breath will put extra stress on your blood vessels. Have a safety spotter present as you exercise. The spotter can prevent accidents by taking the bar from you when you are too tired, or when you have accidentally attempted a weight that is too heavy for you.

REPETITIONS AND SETS

Repetitions are the number of times a specific exercise is done. A set (or bout) is one group of repetitions. For example, if you do five push-ups in a row, that is one set of five repetitions. An isotonic program generally includes three sets of exercises with five to eight repetitions of each exercise every other day.

Weight Training Exercises
Bent-over rowing
Press
Half squats
Bench press

Both isometric and isotonic exercises can produce significant gains in strength in a short period of time. However, of the two, isotonic exercises are used more extensively in programs to develop muscular strength. Isometrics do have an advantage for people who have no access to equipment, or who must exercise in a small space. Many people find they can exercise isometrically during their working hours.

3. Muscular Endurance

Muscular endurance is the capacity to perform an activity for a long time without becoming tired. Muscular strength might enable you to lift a heavy backpack onto your shoulders. However, muscular endurance will enable you to carry the backpack for 30 km without fatigue.

Muscular endurance is important not only in sports but in everyday activities such as sitting, standing, walking, and climbing. Any job requiring the constant repetition of one action (shovelling snow, scrubbing floors, handling baggage, hammering nails) requires a high degree of endurance.

To improve your muscular endurance, it is a good idea to begin with easy exercises such as stride jumping, jogging in place, and lifting and lowering your legs while lying on your side. When you can do these without strain for a sustained length of time, you are ready to advance to chin-ups, speed sit-ups, push-ups, and half-squats. It is better to do two sets of 15 movements

THE STANDARDIZED TEST OF FITNESS

If your school has the proper equipment, you can test all of the different parts of body health. Some of the tests do not require equipment. However, if you want to know accurately the state of your body health, you will have to perform all of the tests.

Cardiorespiratory fitness can be tested by the Canadian Home Fitness Test described in Chapter 2.

Muscular strength can be tested with a hand grip dynamometer.

Muscular endurance can be tested with push-ups or sit-ups.

Flexibility can be tested with a sit and reach apparatus.

Body fat can be tested by using skin-fold calipers.

Your teacher should have information on the normal levels of fitness for people your age.

SOME PROBLEMS IN MUSCULAR ENDURANCE

Hitting the Wall

"I felt sick, tired, and I wanted to lie down. My mind said 'go on' but my legs wouldn't respond." The runner who made this statement had "hit the wall." He had run out of **glycogen** (body fuel) for his muscles. This fuel supply is needed for the muscles to contract and when it is used up, the muscles cannot work. You can, however, train your muscles to store more fuel and thus increase the ability of your muscles to work for a longer period of time.

Oxygen Starvation

"I couldn't seem to get enough air. I was panting so hard my lungs felt like they were going to burst." This athlete was suffering "**oxygen starvation**." This occurs when the muscles are not obtaining enough oxygen to convert the glycogen to energy. Training can help the heart and blood provide more oxygen to the muscles. Exercising the muscles also makes them more efficient so that they require less oxygen.

Lactic Acid Build-Up

When any fuel is burned, there are left-over products. As glycogen is used up, a waste product called **lactic acid** is left in the muscles. Oxygen is needed to eliminate the lactic acid.

If your exercise makes you breathe deeply, but you do not need to gasp for breath, you are said to be exercising aerobically (with oxygen) and there is no accumulation of lactic acid. When you run out of oxygen and gasp for breath, you are said to be exercising anaerobically (without oxygen). It is then that lactic acid accumulates and the muscles start to lose their ability to function. The only way to remove the lactic acid build-up is to rest.

As you rest your body, more oxygen becomes available and the lactic acid is converted to products that are easily eliminated. Experts have found that a light exercise such as walking rather than complete rest will reduce by 50% the amount of time it takes to remove the lactic acid from the blood.

with a short rest in between than to attempt to do 30 movements at once. If you overexercise, you may develop sore muscles.

4. Flexibility

In order to walk, bend, jump, climb, or run, you must be able to move your joints—the points of the body where two bones join—fully and easily. This ability is called **flexibility**.

We have all admired the grace of the gymnast or the fluid motion of the dancer. People with good flexibility move easily and smoothly and are less likely to tire or to injure **ligaments** and muscles. Inactive people often have poor flexibility because their muscles are rarely stretched.

There are two types of flexibility exercise. Passive flexibility exercises involve stretching muscles slowly beyond normal length and then holding that position. This type of exercise is good for warm-ups and for repairing injured muscles.

Active flexibility exercises involve stretching a muscle beyond maximum length, by bouncing against it rhythmically. Although these exercises may be more effective than passive flexibility exercises, they may result in injury to the muscle if they are not done carefully.

Overemphasis on one particular exercise or on one particular muscle group may cause a decrease in flexibility. It is important, therefore, to include flexibility exercises when building strength and endurance.

Toe Reach
(Passive Flexiblity Exercise)

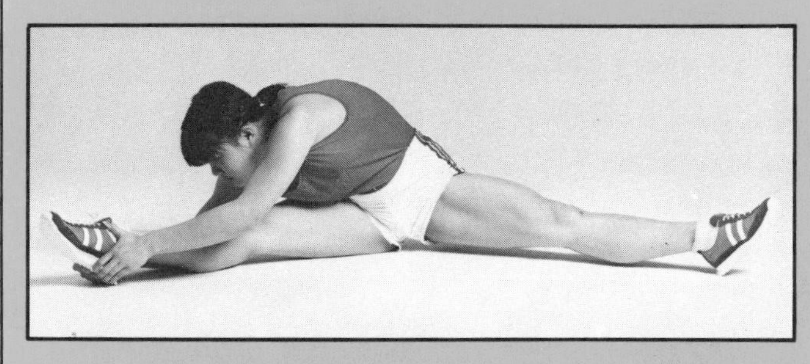

Grasp ankle with both hands and try to touch head to knee, holding it there for 10 seconds.

Side Stretch
(Active Flexibility Exercise)

Gently bounce up and down six times after you have stretched as far as you can.

5. Ideal Body Fat

You can have cardiorespiratory fitness, strength, endurance, and flexibility, and still be physically unhealthy if the proportion of your mass that is body fat is too high. Excess body fat puts extra strain on all of your body systems. For example, your heart has to work harder because it must pump blood through a greater area. You have less energy and you do not look your best.

Proper body mass is such an important aspect of fitness that Chapter 4 will discuss it in detail.

Physical Skills

The second major area of physical fitness consists of five skills that enable you to do well at certain sports, to perform certain jobs, and to respond to emergency situations. All of us need some of these skills in everyday life. Some activities require them more than others and certain kinds of work demand a high degree of expertise. There are people who are simply born with natural ability in these areas; however, you can usually improve your skills if you identify your weaknesses and practise regularly.

1. Agility

Agility is the ability to change the direction and position of your body quickly with control. Sports such as hockey, basketball, soccer, gymnastics and the various martial arts require a high degree of agility.

AGILITY JUMP TEST

See if you can do this test twice without losing your balance.

1. Balance on your right foot on a line.
2. Jump to your left foot, landing to the right of the line.
3. Jump to your right foot, landing on the other side of the line.
4. Jump to your left foot, landing on the line.

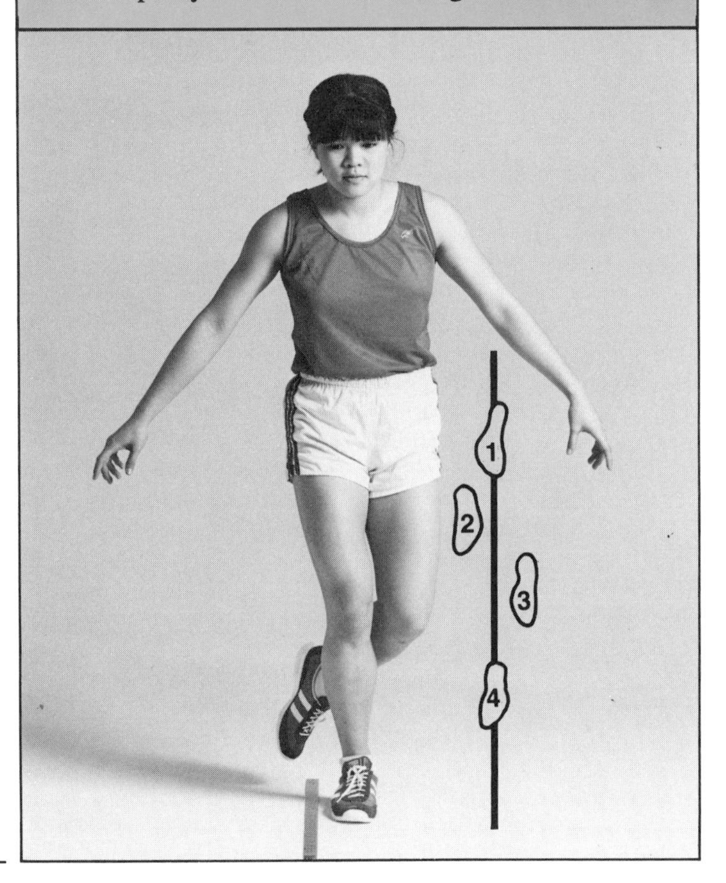

SPEED TEST

A good time for a grade nine student is under 8.5 s.

1. Measure 50 m on a field or track.
2. Use a track start, "On your mark; get set; go."
3. With a stop watch, obtain your time for 50 m.

2. Speed, Reaction Time, and Movement Time

Speed is the ability to perform a movement or to cover a distance in a minimum time. Speed can refer to arm movement (for example, throwing a ball quickly) or to leg movements (for example, running a distance in a short period of time).

Reaction time refers to the time it takes for the brain to perceive the stimulus and send a message to the muscles. **Movement time** refers to the time it takes to activate the muscles. Baseball players need good reaction time to see the ball and to get ready to swing the bat with speed and strength. They also need good movement time to swing the bat at the right moment. Timing is crucial in starts in track and field and swimming, and in sports such as basketball and hockey. By repeating a movement over and over, you can improve reaction time. You can improve movement time by increasing the strength and flexibility of your muscles.

3. Power

Power is the capacity to do strength activities quickly. Sports activities such as shot-put, discus, swimming, high jump, and weight lifting require power. It is also necessary for jobs that involve lifting a load quickly. People who move furniture, lift crates of fruit and vegetables, or raise heavy blocks in construction must be powerful in order to do their work.

REACTION TIME TEST

How fast do you react?

1. Work with a partner. Your partner holds a ruler between your fingers.
2. Your partner drops the ruler and you try to grasp it as quickly as possible.
3. Note how far the ruler has dropped before you grasp it. Does the distance become less with practice?

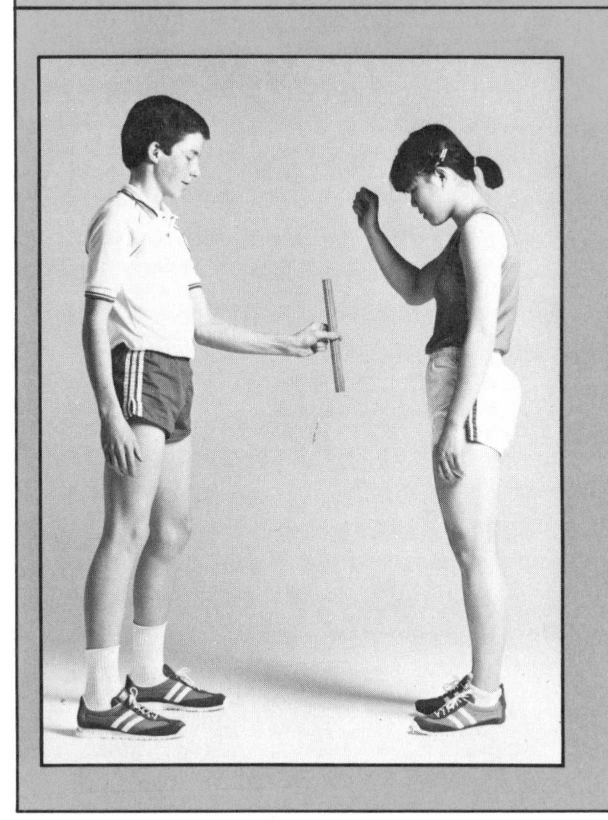

POWER TEST

You will discover if you have strong legs.

1. Kneel so that your toes and knees are on the floor.
2. Hold your arms back and point your toes straight backward.
3. Without curling your toes or rocking your body backward, swing your arms upward and jump to your feet.
4. Hold your position for 3 s once you land.

EYE-HAND CO-ORDINATION TEST

How good is your eye-hand co-ordination?

1. Place a tall bottle with an opening of approximately 5 cm on the floor.
2. Obtain 10 unsharpened pencils.
3. Stand over the bottle, holding a pencil at one end (use first and second fingers).
4. Aim the pencil for the opening and release the pencil.If the pencil goes into the bottle and then bounces out, it is scored as in.
5. A score of four or better indicates good eye-hand co-ordination.

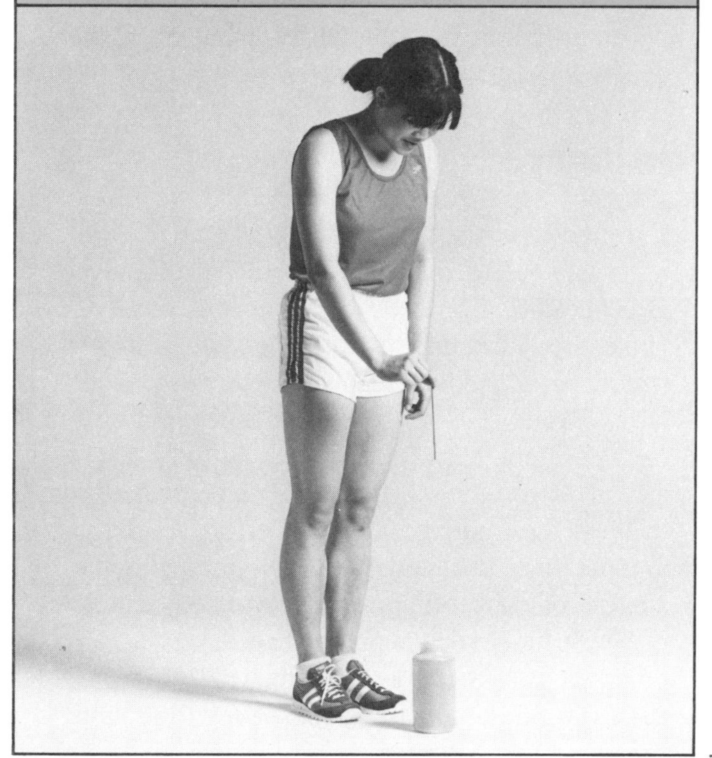

4. Co-ordination

Co-ordination is the ability to use your senses, such as your eyes, together with your arms or legs, or to use two or more body parts at the same time. Co-ordination is quite specific to the activity. Individuals who have good eye-hand co-ordination can hit a volleyball, baseball, or golf ball with ease and accuracy. Sports such as soccer or football require good eye-foot co-ordination. Occupations such as typing, assembly work, drafting, and surgery demand good eye-hand co-ordination.

5. Balance

Balance is the ability to keep the body in a stable position while still or moving. Whether you are involved in sports such as skateboarding, curling, skiing, and surfing or simply learning to ride a bike, a sense of balance is an important skill.

BALANCE TEST

Try the stork-stand balance.

1. Stand on your left foot.
2. Hold the bottom of your right foot against the inside of your left knee.
3. Place your hands on your hips.
4. Shut your eyes and hold this position for 10 s without moving your left foot.

SOME GENERAL PRINCIPLES OF FITNESS TRAINING

You have looked at the basic parts of physical fitness. Before planning a fitness program, you should also understand some of the basic principles of training and conditioning.

Specific Training

Specific training means that you must do certain kinds of activity or exercise to build specific parts of physical fitness. An exercise to improve strength will not necessarily improve flexibility. Similarly, participating in one sport will not necessarily improve your performance in another sport.

Extent of Training

Extent of training is the amount of exercise necessary to improve your fitness. The effectiveness of training depends upon how strenuously you exercise (intensity), how often you exercise (frequency), and how long your exercise period lasts (duration). Overtraining or undertraining can be equally harmful. For exercise to be effective, you should start slowly and gradually increase the amount of time and effort. Each time you put your body under stress by increasing the amount of exercise, you are applying the principle of overload. If you are out of shape, start by doing the activity for a short time (10 to 15 min) each session. Gradually increase your time, until you are doing it for at least half an hour, 3 times a week. As you get into shape, you may want to alternate between hard days when you really put your body through a workout and easy days when you allow your muscles to recover. Easy days are particularly important before an event. Even top athletes need recovery time from competition or hard workouts. The time needed for rest may vary from 24 h for gymnasts to several days for marathon runners.

LIMITS OF SPECIFIC TRAINING

Each year a group of top Canadian athletes from various sports enters a superstars competition at Ontario Place in Toronto. The rules do not allow them to compete in their own sport. Results show that while a person may be highly skilled in one area his or her abilities in other areas are often poor. One hockey star who was exceptional on ice could barely swim 25 m, while a baseball player had trouble finishing the 800 m run.

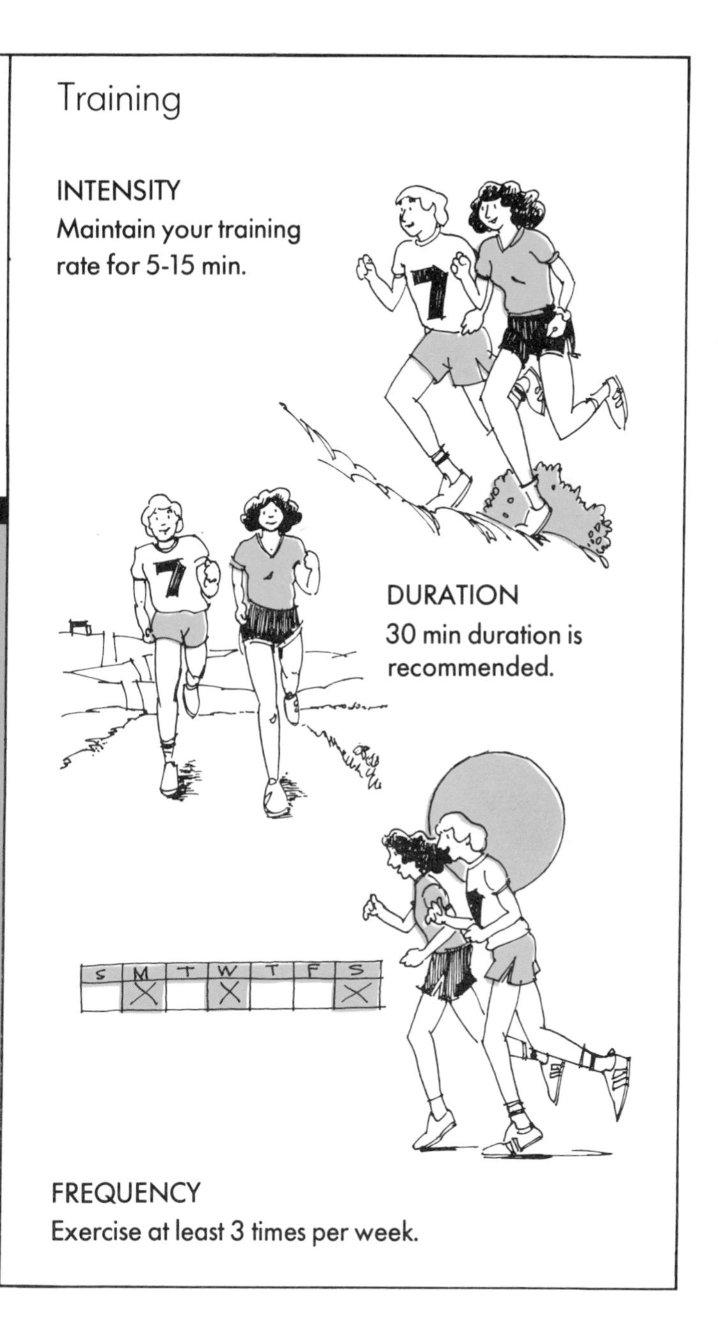

Warm-up and Cool-down

A **warm-up** prepares your body for a workout and is a wise precaution against injury and soreness. It increases the blood flow to your muscles. At the same time your muscles and tendons are stretched in preparation for greater contractions. It also allows a gradual speed-up of your heart so that it is not put under sudden stress.

A **cool-down** after a workout is best achieved by continuing your activity, but at a slower rate. This allows your muscles to help pump blood from the extremities back to the heart and brain. When you stop an activity quickly, the blood sent to the muscles collects there, depriving the brain of oxygen. You may become dizzy and faint.

Be sure to do warm-ups and cool-downs during each exercise session. Do not jump into an activity after sitting all day in school. Do not stop your activity suddenly. Give your body a chance to adjust gradually.

Maintaining Physical Fitness

Even if you have been training for years, you only need a few weeks of inactivity to lose your fitness level. It takes far less time to get out of shape than it takes to become fit. Even professional athletes find that their fitness drops off after three to four weeks if they do not exercise. In order to stay fit you must regularly use your muscles.

WHAT IS A GOOD FITNESS PROGRAM FOR YOU?

Your physical fitness program should improve you in all of the aspects related to body health and in some of those related to physical skills. However, your program should also meet your own interests and abilities. The fitness level you require and the means you choose to achieve it can be quite different from those of someone else.

A few of you may wish to become star athletes; you will require a special fitness program that will train you for the sport you are interested in. However, what most of you want is to be able to go about your daily routine with energy and alertness. You want to feel well and enjoy life. Your fitness program should achieve that for you.

Some of you may already be so constantly "on the go" that you feel you are getting enough exercise. Think about your activities. You can be always busy, but never get the kind of exercise that you really need.

Setting up a fitness program does not have to be complicated. Just pick a vigorous activity or sport that you enjoy—swimming, dancing, hiking, tennis, cycling, skating, rowing. Vigorous activities are ones that involve all major parts of the body—neck, arms, chest, abdomen, back, and legs. If you prefer variety, combine several different activities. Go swimming one day, hiking another day, and dancing the third day (or choose any other combination you like). A combination of these activities will increase your cardiorespiratory fitness and your muscular strength and endurance.

DRUGS AND ATHLETICS

Many weight lifters and competitors in track and field are convinced that steroid drugs are beneficial because they build strength. They can build muscle tissue in conjunction with exercise. However, they also have serious side-effects, particularly in females. Women who take these drugs will develop masculine characteristics which cannot be reversed.

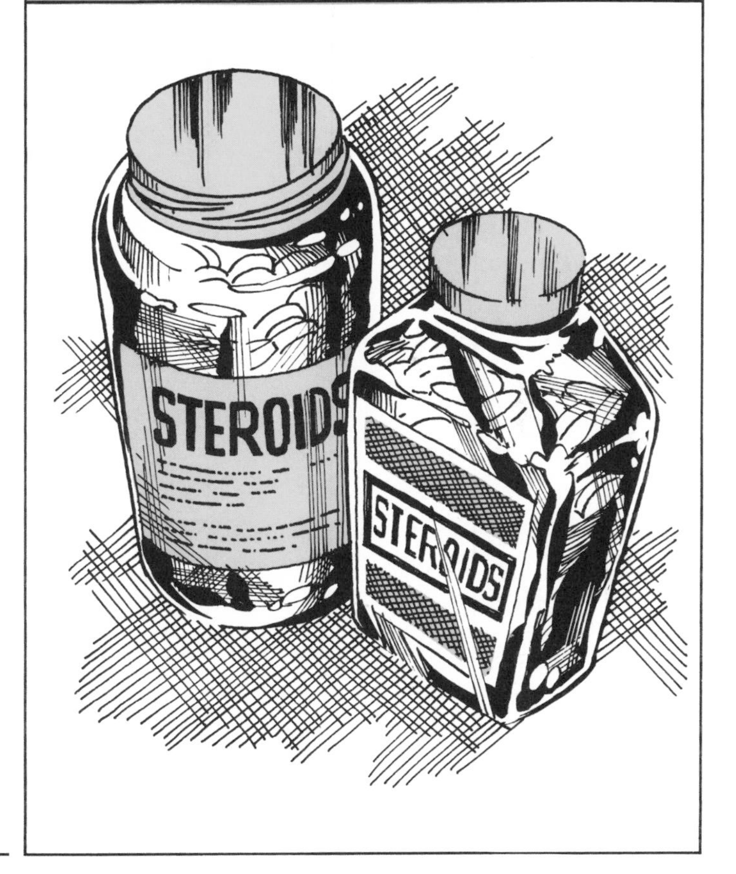

If you are interested in achieving a high level of fitness, your fitness program should include both exercises and activities. Here is a suggested combination:

- an activity that increases cardiorespiratory fitness (jogging, swimming, cycling, etc.)
- some exercises designed to increase the strength and endurance of specific muscles (weight training, speed sit-ups, flexed-arm hangs, etc.)
- passive stretching exercises for flexibility (toe reach, side stretch.)

Some activities are more useful than others in developing physical fitness. Activities to consider for a fitness program are suggested in the following chart, with their estimated effectiveness in promoting body health. If you are out of shape, be realistic about the results you expect. It takes time to get back into condition.

	Cardio-respiratory Fitness	Muscular Strength	Muscular Endurance	Flexibility
Basketball	excellent	poor	good	fair
Bicycling	excellent	good	good	poor
Bowling	poor	poor	poor	poor
Calisthenics	fair	good	fair	excellent
Disco Dancing	good	fair	good	good
Gymnastics	fair	excellent	excellent	excellent
Jogging	excellent	fair	excellent	poor
Ropejumping	excellent	good	excellent	poor
Skating, Ice- or Roller-	good	poor	good	fair
Skiing, Cross-country	excellent	fair	excellent	fair
Skiing, Downhill	fair	fair	fair	fair
Softball	poor	poor	poor	poor
Swimming	excellent	fair	excellent	fair
Table Tennis	poor	poor	poor	poor
Tennis	fair	fair	fair	fair
Volleyball	fair	fair	poor	poor
Walking	good	poor	fair	poor

NOTE: How energetically you perform these activities will affect their ratings.

TWO PLANS FOR FITNESS TRAINING

Circuit training is a method in which you practise an exercise at one location in the gym for a limited time, then move to another location and practise a new exercise. Because you will work at six or more different activities in the circuit, you will improve your cardiorespiratory fitness, muscular endurance, muscular strength, and flexibility.

Interval training is a method in which a period of work is followed by a period of rest. First you run a specific distance in a certain amount of time. Then you walk for a specific distance. For example, you might run 250 m and then walk for 100 m. This is an excellent way to improve your cardiorespiratory fitness.

PHYSICAL FITNESS — A LIFETIME HABIT

Your physical fitness program should be both enjoyable and challenging. Choose activities you like and share them with a friend. If you tire of a sport, try one that tests new skills. Set yourself some fitness goals and work toward them. It takes time and effort to keep fit.

Fitness is more than a program of exercises. It is a way of life. Take whatever opportunities you have each day to use your physical abilities instead of machines. Walk instead of drive. Use the stairs rather than the escalator. Instead of watching television, do a few simple exercises. By making fitness a part of your life now, you will be developing a habit that could last a lifetime.

FOR REVIEW

Key Ideas

- Physical fitness is the ability of the heart, blood vessels, lungs, and muscles to function efficiently.
- Physical fitness can be divided into two general areas: fitness related to the health of your body and fitness related to your ability to perform certain physical skills.
- A physical fitness program should improve your body in all aspects related to health and in some of those related to physical skills.
- General principles of fitness training include: specific training, extent of training, the principle of overload, hard days and easy days, warm-up and cool-down, and maintaining fitness.

Questions and Activities

1. *a.* Identify the aspects of body health that a fitness program will improve.
   b. Identify the physical skills that can be improved through practice.
2. Explain the meaning of specific training, extent of training, warm-up and cool-down.
3. Prepare a checklist of the ways people can increase physical activity in daily life: e.g., parking car at far end of lot, taking stairs instead of escalators, walking or bicycling for short errands, and exercising while watching television. Survey the class to find out how many students try to increase physical activity.
4. Tell why the following are myths about exercise and fitness:
   a. Exercise causes heart trouble.
   b. Exercise should be avoided as you get older.
   c. You can get physically fit by deep breathing, yoga, or **calisthenics** alone.
   d. Women who engage in vigorous exercise and sports become overly muscular.
5. Write a short report on a sport that you enjoy, interview a successful athlete, or write a brief biography of a famous Canadian sports figure. What qualities are necessary for successful participation in sports?

6. Set up a program to develop muscular strength for a sport or activity you prefer.
7. Find out more about the following fitness activities: aqua dynamics, yoga, dancercize, karate, t'ai chi, judo.
8. Plan a general fitness program for yourself for the next three months. Consult the chart on page 34 and discuss your program with your physical education teacher. The program should include warm-ups, a variety of activities to develop all parts of physical fitness, cool-downs, and an evaluation of progress. Draw up a calendar with regular time blocks set aside for this activity.
9. Working with a small group of classmates, choose one of the following students and devise a plan for an intensive fitness program for him or her:
   a. A fourteen-year-old boy with little athletic experience and no regular vigorous activity.
   b. A thirteen-year-old girl who plays softball several times a week all summer.
   c. A fifteen-year-old girl who is on a swim team and who swims almost every day.
   d. A fourteen-year-old boy who has decided to try out for the football team. (He wants to play on the line.)

1565

CHAPTER TWO

YOUR CARDIO RESPIRATORY FITNESS

WHAT IS CARDIORESPIRATORY FITNESS?

Cardiorespiratory fitness involves the health and efficiency of the heart, lungs, and blood vessels. If you have good cardiorespiratory fitness, your heart is able to pump the blood out to the muscles easily and efficiently for long periods of time and your lungs are able to draw enough air into your body to provide oxygen-rich blood for your heart to pump. It is the most important aspect of physical fitness, because it is the chief factor affecting your capacity for physical work. It will determine the amount of work you can do and the length of time you can continue working. In order to improve your cardiorespiratory fitness, you should understand how your cardiorespiratory system works. It involves three essential parts: heart, lungs, and blood vessels.

The thick walls of the heart are composed of interlacing fibres called cardiac muscle. Inside, the heart is made up of four chambers, two at the top (the atria) and two at the bottom (the ventricles). The heart is also divided by a partition with the right **atrium** and right **ventricle** forming one side, and the left atrium and left ventricle forming the other. On each side between the atrium and ventricle are valves through which the blood moves. There are also valves between the ventricles and the arteries into which blood is pumped. These valves prevent the blood from flowing backward into the chambers it has left.

The heart acts as a powerful pump with two functions. When the two atria contract together, the right atrium forces blood containing waste products from the body into the right ventricle. The left atrium forces fresh blood from the lungs into the left ventricle. As the two ventricles contract, the "used" blood from the body travels from the right ventricle into the **pulmonary artery** which carries it to the lungs. There it picks up fresh oxygen. The left ventricle pumps fresh blood, which has come from the left atrium, into the **aorta** and to the body.

Cardiorespiratory fitness determines the amount of work you can do.

THE OPERATION OF THE CARDIORESPIRATORY SYSTEM

STAGE 1 The heart pumps the blood with its waste materials to the lungs to discharge the carbon dioxide and pick up new oxygen.

STAGE 2 The lungs take in air containing oxygen. The alveolar sacs in the lungs have very thin walls which contain networks of tiny capillaries where oxygen is absorbed and carbon dioxide released. The blood carries the fresh oxygen back to the heart.

STAGE 3 The heart pumps the oxygen-fresh blood to the arteries, which carry it to capillaries in all parts of the body.

STAGE 4 Oxygen and nutrients in the blood pass through the capillary walls to nearby cells. Carbon dioxide and other waste products pass from the cells into the blood.

STAGE 5 The blood carries these waste products from the capillaries through venules to veins and back to the heart.
The cycle then repeats itself.

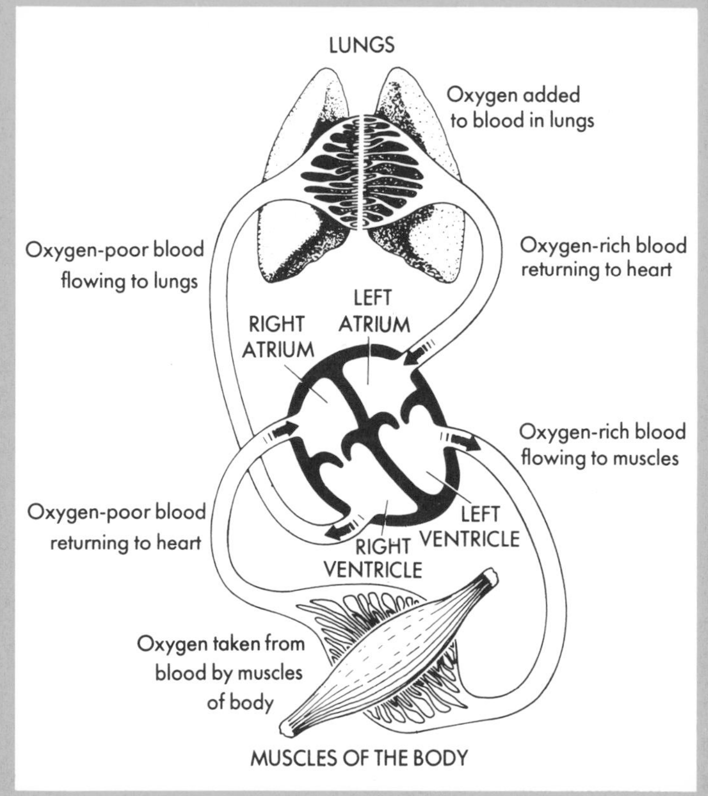

NOTE: The two blood vessels leaving the ventricles are not in the proper location. Because these vessels exist behind the heart their actual position cannot be shown in this diagram.

The heart-lung-heart movement of blood is called the **pulmonary circulation**. The heart-body-heart movement of blood is called the **systemic circulation**.

The lungs, which are in the chest on either side of the heart, also have two functions. They take in fresh oxygen for the body to use and they eliminate carbon dioxide from the body.

The **trachea** or wind pipe divides into two tubes called main **bronchi**, one for each lung. The bronchi then subdivide into smaller and smaller tubes called bronchioles. At the ends of the bronchioles are many tiny air sacs called **alveoli**. Oxygen passes through this network of tubes to the alveoli where the exchange of oxygen and carbon dioxide takes place.

Blood vessels are an essential part of the cardiorespiratory system because they connect the heart and the lungs to the various parts of the body. Arteries are thick-walled muscular vessels which carry blood from the heart throughout the body. The pulmonary artery carries "used" blood to the lungs. The aorta carries oxygen-rich blood to the body. **Veins** are thin-walled vessels that return blood to the heart from various parts of the body. **Capillaries** and **venules** are tiny vessels that form a mesh between the arteries and veins. The transfer of oxygen and carbon dioxide and nutrients and waste products to and from the cells takes place here.

For the cardiorespiratory system to operate effectively, all of its parts must be functioning together properly. A weakness in one part means that the entire system suffers.

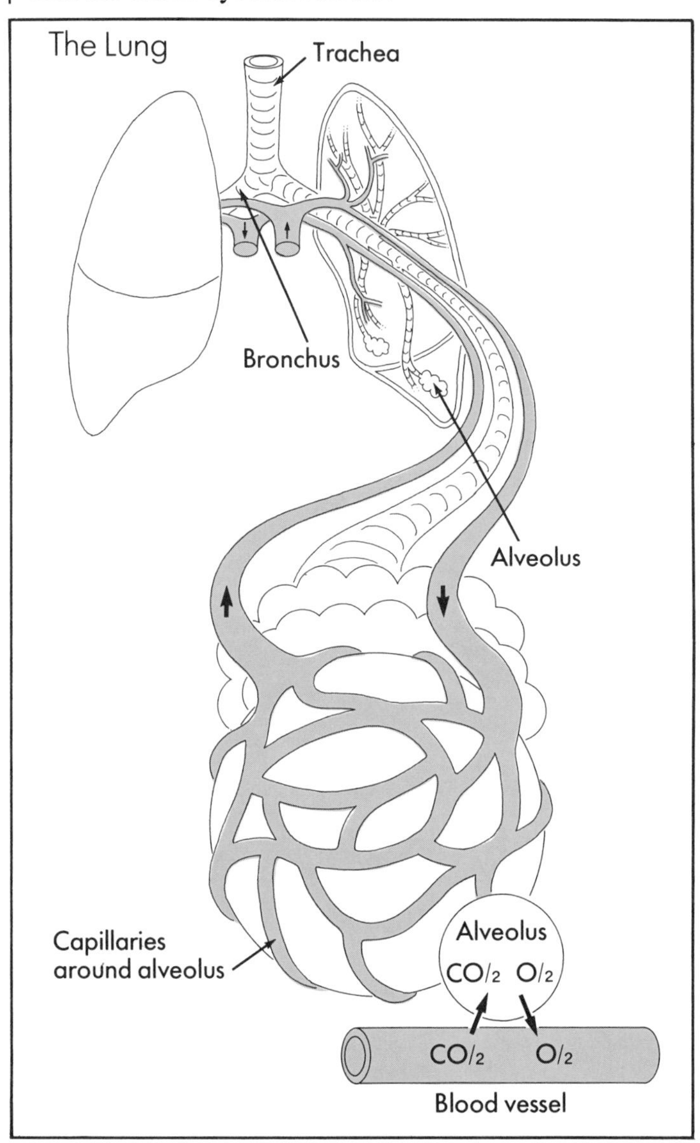

Swimming is an excellent way to improve your cardiorespiratory fitness.

SOME BENEFITS OF CARDIORESPIRATORY FITNESS

Cardiorespiratory fitness will benefit you in a number of important ways:

1. More Efficient Lungs

Regular exercise increases the capacity of the lungs to take in air.

2. Healthier Heart

The heart is a muscle that can be strengthened through exercise. The stronger it is, the more forcibly it can push with each beat and, therefore, the fewer times it needs to beat.

Non-athletes usually have a **pulse rate** of about 70 beats per minute when they are at rest. Long distance runners, however, often have a pulse of 45 or less when at rest. Their hearts are so strong they do not have to beat as often to push the same amount of blood through the system. A heart which is seldom exercised to its fullest capacity is a weak heart; it will have to beat very fast when sudden work or an emergency calls for action. It may not be able to pump enough blood for all of the demands on it. If this happens, a person has heart failure.

3. Healthier Arteries

Healthy arteries and veins are those which are flexible and clear of any deposits which would narrow them. They can expand to accommodate surges of blood. If the arteries become narrow and inflexible, it is difficult for the blood to pass through them. This happens if **cholesterol** deposits are present in the walls of the arteries.

Cholesterol, which is a white waxy substance that is solid at body temperature, can collect on the inner walls of the arteries when there is too much of it in the blood. It is manufactured by the liver and also found in foods such as egg yolks, animal fats and dairy products. The disease associated with cholesterol deposits in the arteries is called **atherosclerosis**. Because this disease hampers the flow of blood through the blood vessels, the heart must work much harder to push the same amount of blood the same distance.

Narrowed arteries are especially dangerous if there is a clot in the blood. A small clot in an **artery** of the heart (**coronary artery**) can stop the flow of blood to the heart and cause a **heart attack**. A clot in an artery in the brain can cause a **stroke**.

Both diet and exercise are important factors contributing to the health of your arteries. Intensive exercise has been shown actually to increase the number of blood vessels in your heart. When a strenuous training program is undertaken, your circulatory system is under stress. Your body reacts by building a better network of blood vessels (**collateral circulation**) to handle the flow of blood. This means that more than one blood vessel will supply blood to a given area of the heart. If one artery becomes blocked, blood will still continue to flow in that section and prevent or reduce the effects of a heart attack.

The Development of Atherosclerosis

Blood vessel wall

NORMAL ARTERY

Deposits in the wall

ATHEROSCLEROSIS

4. Other Benefits

Cardiorespiratory exercise is beneficial in other important ways. It improves your appearance and helps you to control your body mass. Because it leads to greater reserves of physical energy, you can get more work done, faster, with less effort. We all know people who have tremendous vitality and a zest for living. These people have added a quality to their lifestyle that others admire.

TWO WAYS TO TAKE YOUR PULSE

Neck Pulse (Carotid Pulse)

Place your thumb lightly on one side of your Adam's apple and your fingers on the other side. You should be able to feel the pulse of the carotid artery. If you do not feel it, move your fingers slightly to one side or the other until you feel it. Press lightly so you do not cut off circulation.

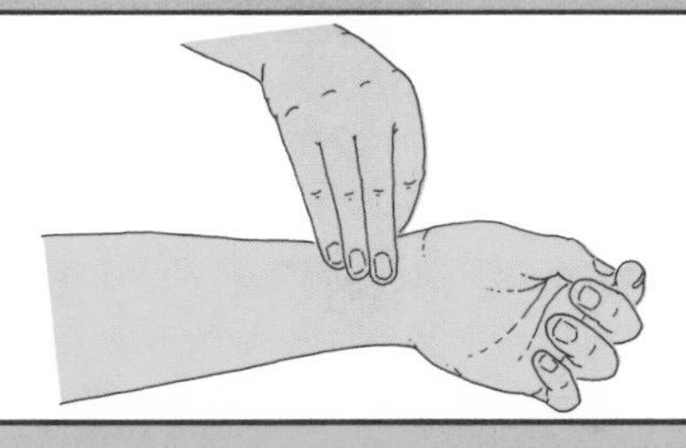

Wrist Pulse

Hold your left hand in front of you, wrist up. Place the first and second fingers of your right hand on your left wrist (to the left, or thumb side, of the double tendon running down the centre of the wrist) about 2 cm down from the hand. Press gently until you feel a pulse.

TESTING YOUR CARDIORESPIRATORY SYSTEM

Is your cardiorespiratory system in as good shape as you would like it to be or as it should be? You may feel fine, but this is not a good indication of cardiorespiratory fitness. To determine fitness, special tests that require **stamina** are required. Two such tests are the Step Test and the 12 min Run/Walk.

The Step Test

The object of this test is to see how fast your heart will beat after 3 min of stepping up and down.

To do the Step Test, you need a bench, block, or step about 30 cm high, and a watch with a second hand.

1. Have a partner take your pulse and record it before you begin.
2. Stand in front of the bench or step.
3. Step up with your right foot, then up with your left foot.
4. Step down with your right foot, then down with your left foot.
5. Repeat this 4-count stepping (up, up, down, down) 24 times/min (2 times every 5 s) for 3 min.
6. Sit down and immediately have a partner take your neck pulse for 1 min. If you do not have a partner, take your own pulse at the neck or wrist.

The Step Test

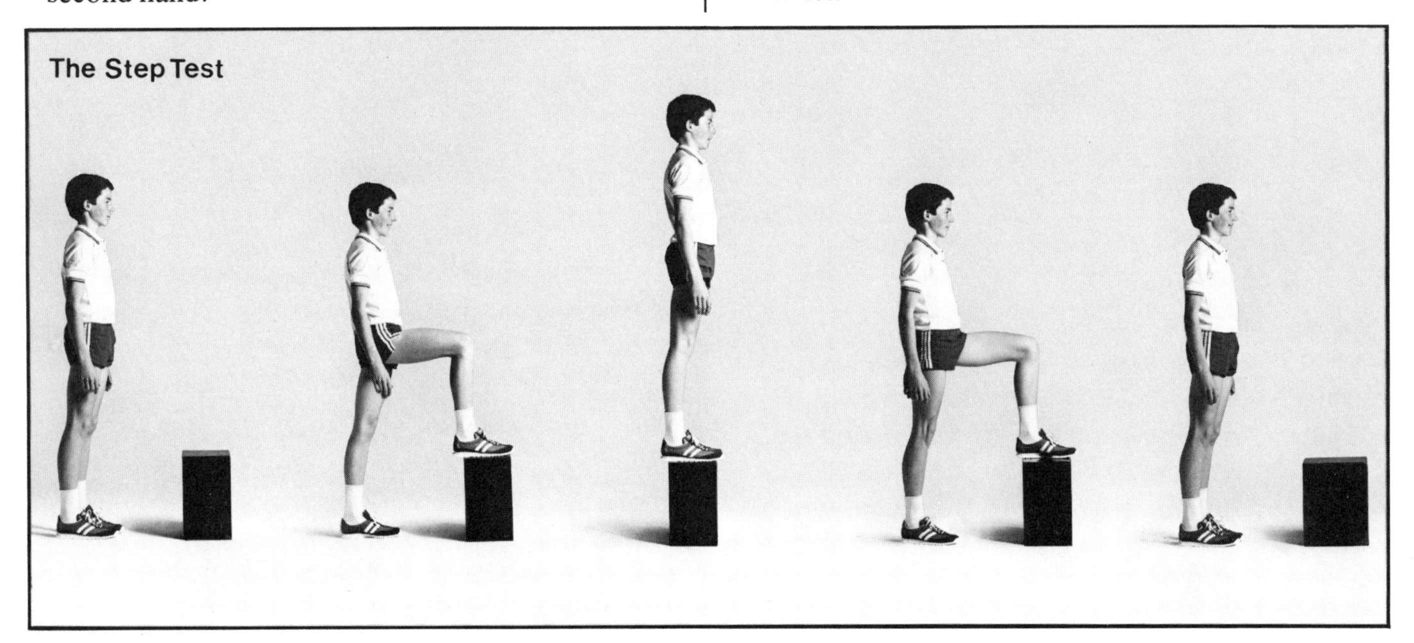

Use the following chart to find your own cardio-respiratory fitness rating. Are you satisfied with your score?

Heart Beats per Minute

Age 13–14		Age 15–16		
Boys	**Girls**	**Boys**	**Girls**	**Cardiorespiratory Fitness Rating**
90 or less	100 or less	85 or less	95 or less	excellent
91–98	101–110	86–95	96–105	good
99–120	111–130	96–115	106–125	fair
above 120	above 130	above 115	above 125	poor

The heart of a person who is fit will return to its normal rate more quickly than that of a person who is not. The time it takes for your heart to return to its normal rate is called the recovery rate.

The 12 min Run/Walk

The purpose of the 12 min Run/Walk is to see how far you can go in the allotted time. In this test, no one sets the pace for you—you try as hard as you want. The test result can be a measure of your fitness, but it can also be a measure of your willingness to try hard. You should do your best so that you will know the level of your cardiorespiratory fitness. However, do not over-work yourself. You are not running a race. To do this test you need a measured place to run (a gym or track) and a watch with a second hand. Have someone be timekeeper for you. This person might also keep track of the number of laps you do.

1. When the signal is given, begin to run at a pace you think you can keep up for a long time.
2. Run at this pace as long as you can, but slow down to a walk when you have to.
3. Run again when you can.
4. At the 12 min signal, stop and compute how many metres you ran.

Use the following chart to determine your cardiorespiratory fitness rating:

Rating Chart: 12 min Run/Walk

NUMBER OF METRES RUN

Rating	13–14 years Boys	13–14 years Girls	15–16 years Boys	15–16 years Girls
Excellent	2750	1925	2825	2100
Good	2425	1750	2550	1925
Fair	2275	1650	2375	1750
Poor	2200	1550	2275	1550

If your rating for either test is fair or poor, or if you could not complete a test, you should consider a program to improve your cardio-respiratory fitness. Some suggestions for planning a program will be given at the end of this chapter.

Laboratory Evaluation of Cardiorespiratory Fitness

The best measurements of cardiorespiratory fitness are obtained in a laboratory under professional supervision. A person's heart beat at rest is first taken by an **electrocardiogram**. Then the person is given a physical stress exercise (usually on a stationary bicycle or treadmill) and the electrocardiogram is repeated. A doctor interprets the readings and determines how fit the cardio-respiratory system is.

PHYSICAL ACTIVITY READINESS TEST

For most people physical activity should not pose any problem or hazard. This test has been designed to identify the small number of individuals for whom physical activity should be restricted or modified.

Answer yes or no to the following symptoms:

1. any known heart trouble
2. frequent pains in chest or heart
3. feel faint or severe dizziness often
4. bone or joint problem, or severe joint pain
5. any other physical reason that would limit activity

If you answered:

YES

—to one or more of these questions, phone or see a physician before increasing physical activity and/or taking a physical test

NO

—to all questions you have reasonable assurance that you could do:

- A graduated exercise program
- An exercise test

THE CANADIAN HOME FITNESS TEST

The Canadian Home Fitness Test was developed by the Minister of State Fitness and Amateur Sport so that Canadians could test their cardio-respiratory fitness in their own homes. It involves stepping up and down to music on two steps that are each 20 cm in height. The tempo of the music differs according to the age and sex of the participants. A complete Fit-Kit includes the music and instructions for this test.

Practise your stepping, using two steps at the bottom of any staircase or use your self-constructed unit.

START: Stand in front of the first step, feet together.

STEP: Place your right foot up on the first step.

STEP: Bring your left foot right up to the second step.

UP: Bring your right foot up on the second step, feet together. Do not turn around.

STEP: Start down with your left foot to the first step.

STEP: Bring your right foot down to the ground level.

DOWN: Bring your left foot to the ground level, feet together.

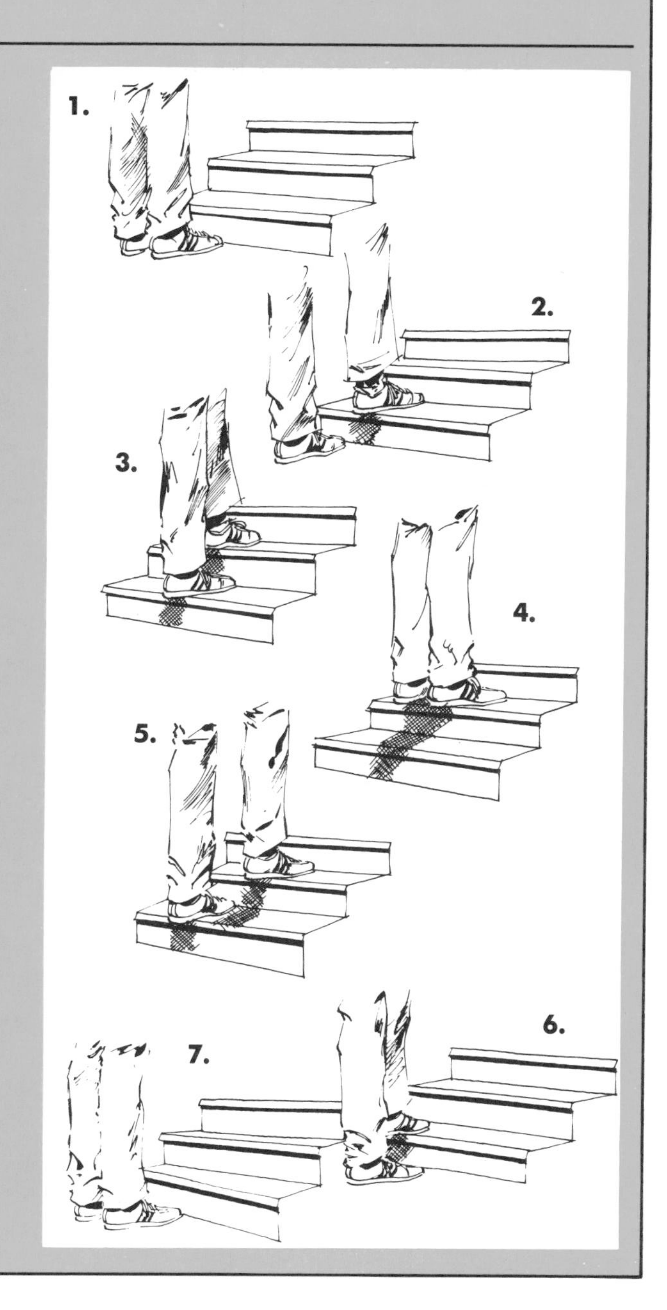

MAINTAINING A HEALTHY CARDIORESPIRATORY SYSTEM

The factors which affect the health of the cardiorespiratory system are: the amount of exercise you get, whether you smoke, what your diet is, and how much stress you are under. Exercise can improve the health of the lungs and heart. Smoking, diet, and stress can contribute to **hypertension** or high blood pressure which means the heart has to work much harder to pump blood. Smoking will also reduce the ability of the lungs to function efficiently.

Exercise

It may be difficult for you to believe that exercising and taking care of yourself now are important for your future. You should be concerned, however, because cardiorespiratory disease often starts very early in life. Examinations of young people killed in accidents or war have found that many 20-year-olds have blood vessels already up to 50% closed by atherosclerosis.

The amount of vigorous exercise people do is one of the most important elements in their cardiorespiratory fitness. Vigorous exercise expands the lungs, strengthens heart muscle, and builds extra blood vessels.

Smoking

Smoking has a direct and devastating effect on your health. Your chances of getting heart disease or respiratory disease increase with the number of cigarettes smoked daily.

Cigarette smoke affects the health of the lungs. Tars from cigarettes damage the lungs, making the transfer of oxygen and carbon dioxide less efficient. Cigarette tar contains small amounts of

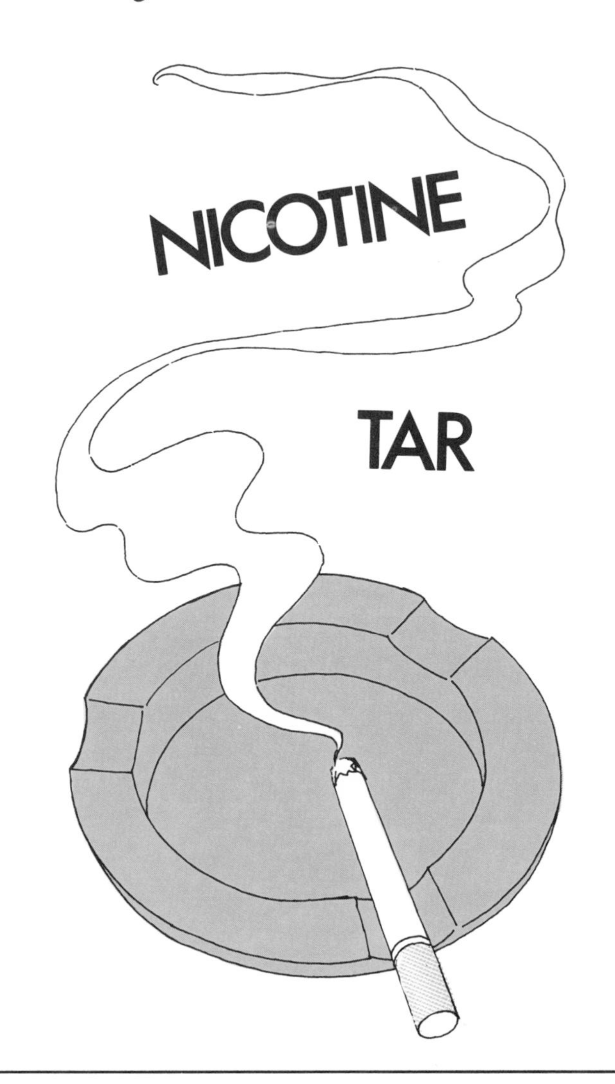

deadly **carcinogens** and materials that may encourage the growth of cancer cells.

The nicotine in cigarettes and the carbon monoxide produced by smoking have been linked to other cardiorespiratory disease. Some doctors believe that nicotine causes greater amounts of fatty material to collect on the inside of blood vessels. It may also increase clotting of the blood and is thought to be a cause of atherosclerosis. Emphysema and **chronic bronchitis** are two respiratory diseases that, in the past, were uncommon. However, today these diseases are reaching epidemic proportions. Cigarette smoking has been identified as the most important cause of both.

Emphysema occurs when the alveoli in the lungs lose their elasticity. This elasticity normally allows these sacs to expand and contract and, therefore, helps in the exchange of oxygen and carbon dioxide. When these sacs are unable to expand, the exchange of oxygen and carbon dioxide between the blood and lungs cannot happen efficiently. Typically, the patient develops shortness of breath and an overworked heart. In chronic bronchitis, the membrane lining the bronchi becomes inflamed. There is excessive production of mucus in the bronchi and bronchioles. This causes the chronic cough typical of chronic bronchitis.

You can greatly reduce your chances of contracting these diseases if you do not smoke.

EXERCISE AND HEART ATTACKS

Exercise is not only recommended to prevent heart attacks, it is also used by some doctors to treat victims of heart attacks. Dr. Terence Kavanagh of Toronto established a long distance jogging program for patients who had had heart attacks. The program was so successful that he brought eight of these people to compete in the Boston Marathon. Seven of them finished and none of them suffered adverse effects.

Diet

Some medical people believe that cholesterol in combination with other factors contributes to atherosclerosis. In North America, where the daily intake of cholesterol-rich foods is high, the incidence of heart disease is also high. In countries like Japan, where there is a low cholesterol diet, the incidence of heart disease is low.

Because of the strong suspicions about cholesterol, you might want to decrease your cholesterol intake as much as you can. You can do this by avoiding fatty foods. Cut down on beef, pork, and eggs. Eat fewer fried foods, such as french fries. Drink skim milk instead of whole milk and eat fewer sweet, sugary foods.

The more extra body mass you have, the more likely you are to get heart disease. For every kilogram of excess fat, the heart must work proportionately harder.

Stress

Stress can affect your cardiorespiratory health. Some doctors believe that stress causes constricting of the blood vessels and therefore contributes to high blood pressure. Because stress can damage the body, you should learn how to relieve it.

Avoid fatty foods.

BLOOD PRESSURE

Blood must be pushed with a certain amount of force or pressure to make it circulate throughout the body. The powerful heart muscle creates this force or pressure by its rhythmic contractions. Contract, relax, contract, relax, contract, relax— that is what is happening when you hear a heart beat or feel your pulse. As the blood is forced along the arteries and capillaries, the walls of the blood vessels offer greater or less resistance, depending on how healthy they are.

These two factors, the contractions of the heart and the resistance of the blood vessels, determine the blood pressure level. Changes in your blood pressure happen according to whether you are active or at rest, excited or calm, sick or well. If your heart has to work very hard and the blood vessels offer much resistance, your blood pressure level will be high. When it remains consistently high, it is called high blood pressure or hypertension, and it is a danger to health.

Blood pressure has two readings: the higher is **systolic pressure** and measures the pressure at the moment the heart beats; the lower is **diastolic pressure** and measures the pressure when the heart is at rest. A reading for a young male is normally about 16.0 kPa systolic and 10.7 kPa diastolic. For a young female the reading should be about 14.7 kPa systolic and 9.3 kPa diastolic. These readings may fluctuate with the time of day, your body position, and the amount of activity you are engaged in at the moment of testing.

Activities to Improve Your Cardiorespiratory Fitness

Exercises that push the heart and lungs beyond their normal capacity so that the heart and the lungs begin to adapt to doing greater work are said to have a **training effect**.

How do you know when exercise is having a training effect? To know this, you have to measure your **heart rate**. If you are just sitting reading a book, you are "at rest", and your pulse rate is probably between 60 and 90 beats per minute. To achieve a training effect, your pulse rate should be made to rise, while exercising, to a point much higher. That point differs for each age group. The formula for finding your own range is as follows:

- your heartbeat should be above 170 minus your age (lower limit)
- your heartbeat should be below 200 minus your age (upper limit)

For example, if you are 14, your minimum exercise heart rate would be 170 – 14, or 156, and your maximum exercise heart rate would be 200 – 14, or 186. Your exercise heart rate would have to be between 156 and 186 beats per minute to have a training effect.

To monitor your heart rate, take your pulse for 15 s (count the first beat as zero). Then multiply that number by 4 to obtain the rate for 1 min.

CARDIORESPIRATORY FITNESS: A LIFETIME HABIT

For the exercise to be effective, you should exercise until you reach the training effect for 5-15 min three times a week. This should be done on alternate days. Each exercise session should follow this pattern: start with a warm-up of at least 5 min to relax and increase flexibility; begin the exercise slowly but increase the intensity as you move; then cool down for at least 5 min.

The best kinds of activities to achieve a training effect are called **aerobics**. Aerobic exercises require great quantities of oxygen and use the large body muscles, particularly the legs. Remember that you may have to do some of these activities more vigorously to reach the desired heart rate. Check your heart rate for the training effect for each activity that you do.

Here are some aerobic activities that could produce the training effect:

- jogging 3 km
- 15 to 20 min of running on the spot
- 60 min of basketball
- cycling 8 km
- swimming 15 to 20 min
- 35 min of cross-country skiing
- 50 min of tennis (singles, players of similar ability)
- 100 min of water-skiing or downhill skiing
- 90 to 120 min of ice-skating or roller-skating
- 60 min of fast dancing
- 60 min of hockey
- 15 to 20 min of skipping rope

Keep up your cardiorespiratory fitness. Finding an exercise or activity that is rewarding and fun for you will make it easier to continue. Exercising with family members or friends may help you to stay with a regular schedule and might be more pleasant than exercising alone. Since your goal is personal fitness, do not compare yourself to anyone else. You are an individual with unique needs and capacities. Remember, too, that even if you have achieved some measure of cardiorespiratory fitness, it can be lost quickly if you do not maintain your program.

Seriously consider not smoking for the rest of your life. You will be doing yourself and others around you a great favour. Adopt a balanced diet that is low in cholesterol. When you are under stress, relieve it with exercise and relaxation. Have your blood pressure checked periodically.

THE ATHLETIC HEART BEATS BETTER

Because the athlete's heart is so muscular, it can pump the same amount of blood with 50 beats per minute that the average heart pumps with 75 beats per minute. Thus, the athlete's heart will beat 13 million fewer times per year.

A healthy body is a great asset. It makes it possible for you to do all the things you want to do. It is worth all the effort and hard decisions you make now.

Exercising with others may help you stay with a regular schedule.

FOR REVIEW

Key Ideas

- Cardiorespiratory fitness is the most important aspect of physical fitness because it is necessary before you can do many activities well.
- Benefits of cardiorespiratory fitness include more efficient lungs, a healthier heart, and healthier arteries and veins.
- To determine cardiorespiratory fitness, special tests that require stamina must be taken.
- The factors which affect the health of the cardiorespiratory system are exercise, smoking habits, diet, and stress.
- To improve cardiorespiratory fitness, exercises must have a training effect.

Questions and Activities

1. Explain the effect of exercise on the lungs and heart.
2. Explain how *a.* smoking, *b.* diet and *c.* stress can affect the health of the cardiorespiratory system.
3. Explain the meaning of training effect.
4. What are the most popular sports and activities that students participate in at school? Do these activities improve the cardiorespiratory system? Why or why not?
5. Rank order the following activities as to their effectiveness in cardiorespiratory fitness—calisthenics, running, bowling, rope-jumping, swimming, weight lifting, slimnastics, judo, isometrics, yoga, and walking.
6. Give a cardiorespiratory test (i.e., Step Test or 12 min Run/Walk) to an athlete and a non-athlete and note the difference in the recovery rate. Take the heart rate before and immediately after the test.
7. Research and report to the class on the effects of jogging on the following:
   a. lower level of cholesterol
   b. reduced rate of heart attacks
   c. recovery of heart attack victims
   d. strengthening of the heart muscle
   e. efficient exchange of oxygen and carbon dioxide.

8. Demonstrate in an experiment how the heart rate changes by taking the pulse rate after 30 s, 1 min, and 2 min of jogging. Note how a plateau effect takes place.

CHAPTER THREE

YOU AND YOUR ACTIVE LIFE

PREVENTION OF INJURIES

Most physical activities involve some risk of injury. If you lead an active life you should know how to protect yourself. In general, the greater the risk involved, the more precautions you should take. For example, sports such as mountain climbing and speed skating require extensive conditioning and training. Contact sports such as hockey and football require both conditioning and training, as well as elaborate protective equipment. By knowing your sport, being physically fit, and using your common sense, you can reduce your chances of being hurt.

You should take preventive measures before, during, and after an activity. The following simple steps can help you to avoid injuries:

1. Before an Activity

Choose clothing and equipment that is appropriate for the type of activity, your body shape and size, and the environment and weather. Sports clothing should be comfortable and practical. Hats and porous clothing can prevent heat stroke and heat exhaustion on hot days. During winter activities you require layers of clothing in order to regulate your body temperature. As you increase your activity your body will heat up. You may want to remove a layer of clothing in order to feel comfortable. As you begin to slow down your body will also cool. You will want to put on your extra layer of clothing to avoid becoming chilled.

Choose appropriate clothing and equipment.

When choosing clothing and equipment you should consider any problems you may have in your body structure. Some of the more common problems include feet with arches that are too high or too low (flat feet), legs that are bowed in (knock-kneed) or bowed out (bow-legged), and legs that are unequal in length. Medical advice is often necessary because a particular defect can add stress to other parts of the body and increase the chance of serious injury. If protective equipment is needed, it should meet the standards of recognized organizations such as the Canadian Standards Association.

A warm-up prior to any strenuous activity should include a slow jog or similar activity followed by stretching activities to prevent injury. The exercises illustrated (pages 62-63) are recommended for 30 to 60 s duration each.

2. During an Activity

Be aware of warning signals from your body when you are active. Mild pain, for example, indicates that a problem exists. Continuing the activity may result in a more serious problem. Muscle stiffness indicates that you have overworked your muscles. In short, you have demanded too much too soon. You can overcome stiffness by rest, light exercise, and slow stretching exercises. Stretches should not be done in a jerky fashion.

Participating in physical activity during very high or low temperatures is unhealthy and your

THE CANADIAN STANDARDS ASSOCIATION

The Canadian Standards Association was founded in 1919 by a group of civil engineers in Montreal. The Standards Division has over 5000 volunteers working in committees that decide performance and safety requirements for products. These standards cover products in 34 fields, including bicycles, hockey helmets, child-resistant packaging, and electrical items. The Certification Division tests products to find out if they meet the requirements. If they do, the manufacturer is licensed to use the CSA mark. Plants are inspected to make sure the products continue to comply with the standards. As well, inspectors bring in merchandise from stores to test. Consumers who are unhappy with a product approved by the CSA can telephone to complain.

body will let you know! If you ignore the warning signs and symptoms, you may suffer from **hypothermia**, frost bite, heat exhaustion, or heat stroke.

3. After an Activity

The cool-down part of an activity is as important as the warm-up in the prevention of injuries. The cool-down follows the same pattern as the warm-up, with stretching exercises and slow simulation of the activity just finished.

In order for your body to repair and replace cells injured by activity, it needs adequate rest and good nutrition. The amount of rest you require will vary with the activity and with your body health. You can find out about the food elements needed for good health in Chapter 4. A book called *Canada's Food Guide*, which is available free from the Federal Department of Health and Welfare, will tell you how to eat meals that contain all of the required nutrients.

If you follow all of the suggestions given above, you will enjoy your activity more and minimize the possibility of injury.

Stretching Exercises to Prevent Muscle Injuries

A. Toe Touch

1. Place your heels together and keep your legs straight.
2. Bend at the waist and try to touch the floor with your fingertips. Do not bounce.
3. Hold this position for a count of ten and then release.
4. Repeat five times.

B. The Plow

1. Lie on your back.
2. Without bending your knees bring your legs over your head.
3. Try to touch the ground with your toes.
4. Hold for a count of ten.
5. Lower your legs and repeat five times.

C. The Back Leg Stretch

1. Face a wall, standing about 1 m away.
2. Place your palms on the wall.
3. Keeping your back straight, and your feet in place, bend your elbows so that your upper body moves closer to the wall.
4. Hold this position for a count of ten.
5. Straighten your arms and repeat five times.

A DANGEROUS RACE

The Marathon race of 42.2 km at the 1978 Pan American Games in San Juan turned out to be a real ordeal for the runners. The event was held at mid-day with temperatures exceeding 30°C.

The effect on some runners was potentially dangerous. Winning times were 10 to 15 min slower than usual and a few contestants complained of water loss and associated heat problems. A Canadian who finished third, to win the bronze medal, lost about 4 L of water during the race. This is just about the limit a human can lose without suffering severe physical problems.

Another Canadian, who finished seventh, stopped perspiring during the run. This was a sign to him that he had reached the danger point. In this condition his body temperature could start rising at an alarming rate and a heat stroke would result. Fortunately, he recognized his symptoms and stopped to take three glasses of water. He proceeded at a slower pace with frequent water stops and was able to finish.

This race was a dramatic example of the perils of exercising in hot, humid weather. During this type of weather, it is recommended that you drink 225 to 350 mL of fluid every 10 to 15 min.

Running at your own pace is the best way.

COMMON INJURIES AND TREATMENT

If you are participating in physical education classes or recreational sports, you may experience a variety of minor injuries. You can prevent these ailments by understanding their causes and taking steps to avoid them.

Blisters

Blisters will occur when socks, shoes, gloves or other equipment rub continually against the skin. They occur most often on the feet. If you do get a blister, drain the fluid with a sterile needle, cover with antiseptic cream, and protect the area from further rubbing with a bandage. Blisters can become infected. If you notice red streaks or experience a lot of discomfort, you should see a doctor immediately. You can prevent blisters by wearing socks and shoes that fit properly and by using the right equipment. If you are prone to blisters, you might rub petroleum jelly inside your shoes at the point where friction is occurring or wear two pairs of socks.

Athlete's Foot

Athlete's foot occurs most often between the fourth and fifth toes because they are pressed closely together in your shoes. This ailment is caused by a fungus which makes the skin dry, scaly, and itchy. You can treat it with sprays and ointments available without prescription from a drug store. To prevent athlete's foot, dry your feet properly after swimming, showering, or exercise when the feet have perspired.

Plantar Warts

Plantar warts, which develop on the soles of the feet, are caused by a **virus**. You get them by walking barefoot where someone who has plantar warts has walked. Since they can multiply quickly and spread to other people, you should see a doctor if you get one.

Jock Itch

Jock itch is a red rash that develops in the groin and on the upper inner part of the thighs. A fungus generally causes this rash and you can treat it with non-prescription medication from the drugstore. If the condition continues after about ten days, you should see a doctor. You can prevent jock itch by changing your underclothes after an activity that has made you perspire heavily.

Abrasions and Lacerations

An **abrasion** is a scrape or cut that occurs on the surface of the skin. You should try to clean the wound thoroughly with water to avoid infection but, if dirt is deeply imbedded, you may have to consult a doctor. Put an antibiotic ointment over the clean wound (you don't need a prescription), and if possible leave the cut open. If the abrasion has to be covered, put a piece of gauze lightly over the area and remove it when you go to bed.

A **laceration** is a deeper cut which may bleed heavily. With an injury like this, controlling the bleeding (see page 76) should be your first concern. You should also consult a doctor because you may need stitches and a **tetanus** shot.

Muscle Cramps

Muscle cramps are very painful. To relieve a cramp, you must stretch or apply pressure to the affected muscle to return it to a normal position. For example, if the cramp occurs in the thigh, press the muscle against a hard surface to push it back in place. For a cramp in the calf muscle, press down on the muscle while pulling up on the toe. Some people believe a deficiency of the mineral potassium is one cause of muscle cramps. To ensure that you have an adequate supply of this mineral, you should eat fresh fruits like bananas or oranges and green leafy vegetables regularly.

Stitches

You may experience pain in the abdomen or side after prolonged exercise such as running. This pain is known as a stitch. People believe this pain happens when the large muscle wall separating the abdomen from the chest has cramped. When this occurs, you should slow down your activity and take slow, deep breaths until it disappears. You can also raise your arm on the affected side and take quick, shallow breaths. You may help to prevent stitches by not eating immediately before exercise.

Muscle Pulls and Tears

You will experience a **muscle pull** or tear when your muscle is stretched beyond its capacity. You may actually feel a "pop" and there may be bleeding in the area of the tear. First aid treatment consists of ice applied at short intervals, compression, and elevation of the injured area. Be sure to consult a doctor.

A muscle pull is the result of a muscle not ready to do the work required. Muscles should be prepared for strenuous exercise by an adequate warm-up.

Tendonitis

The tendon is a strong fibrous material that attaches the muscle to the bone. Though the tendon is an extension of the muscle, it does not contract.

Tendonitis is an inflammation or swelling of the tendon. Unlike many other injuries, it hurts more when you are resting than when you are exercising. Some people make the mistake of

Avoiding injury can be important to your team's success.

continuing to exercise. As a result, they damage the tendon further.

To treat tendonitis, you must first stop the activity that is causing the pain. When the pain begins to disappear, you may want to try a few warm-up exercises. Slow stretching is an effective treatment (see page 62.) You may also want to begin slowly exercising again. If tendonitis returns, consult a doctor.

Ruptured Tendon

When the tendon tears away from the bone or muscle it is said to be ruptured. You will want to see a doctor immediately because the pain of this injury is very intense. You should apply ice, compression, and elevation until you can get medical help.

Shin Splint

Shin splint is much like tendonitis and usually occurs to the sheath just outside the main bone (tibia) of the lower leg. It is a common complaint of runners. It may develop when you continue to run on a hard surface such as pavement or in shoes which do not have good soles for shock absorption. Appropriate treatment includes rest, cold compresses, specific stretching and strengthening exercises, and better shoes.

WHAT TO LOOK FOR IN A JOGGING SHOE

Ideally, jogging shoes should have a rounded, well padded, shock-absorbent arch support and heel. They should be light and flexible, of a porous material such as nylon, with double-stitched seams, durable polyurethane or rubber-compound soles and a protective toecap. A flared heel, wider than the actual foot, gives better stability and ground contact. A good shoe absorbs shock and prevents injury to the knee and ankle.

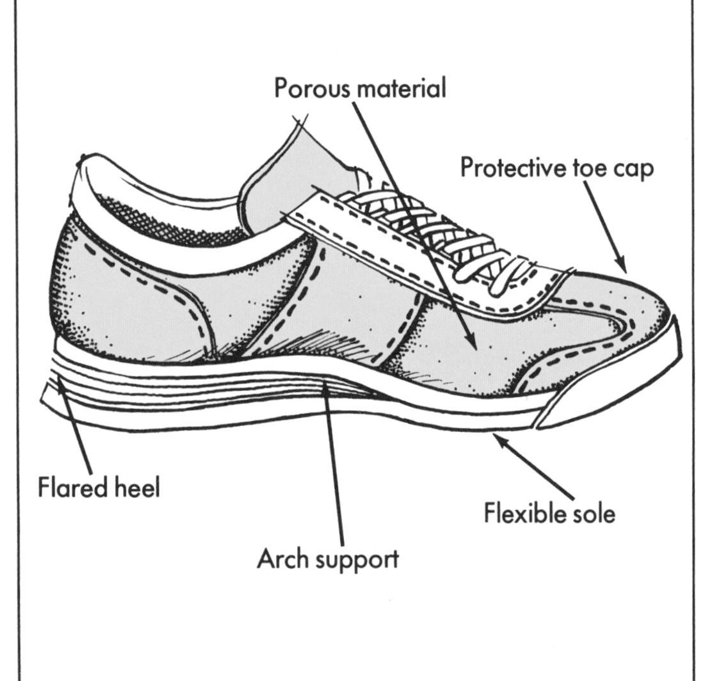

SERIOUS INJURIES

Most of the serious injuries that occur during physical activity involve bones, joints, head, neck, and face. Fortunately, with knowledge and proper use of equipment, some of these injuries can be prevented.

Broken Bones

A broken bone or fracture occurs when a bone of the body breaks, splinters or cracks. A simple fracture is a broken bone with no break in the skin. A compound fracture causes a break in the skin and, therefore, control of bleeding is your first concern. Treatment for broken bones is discussed on page 76.

Joint Injuries

A **joint** is the area between two bones that allows the bones to move in relationship to one another. Joints are made up of the following parts:

- **cartilage**, a tough white gristle which covers the ends of the bones and protects the bones from rubbing against each other;
- a fluid which acts as a lubricant;
- ligaments which are strong fibrous bands that join one bone to another and keep the joint intact.

Because joints are the focal points for body movement, serious injuries commonly occur there. Joints are not as strong as the surrounding bones and are less able to withstand stress.

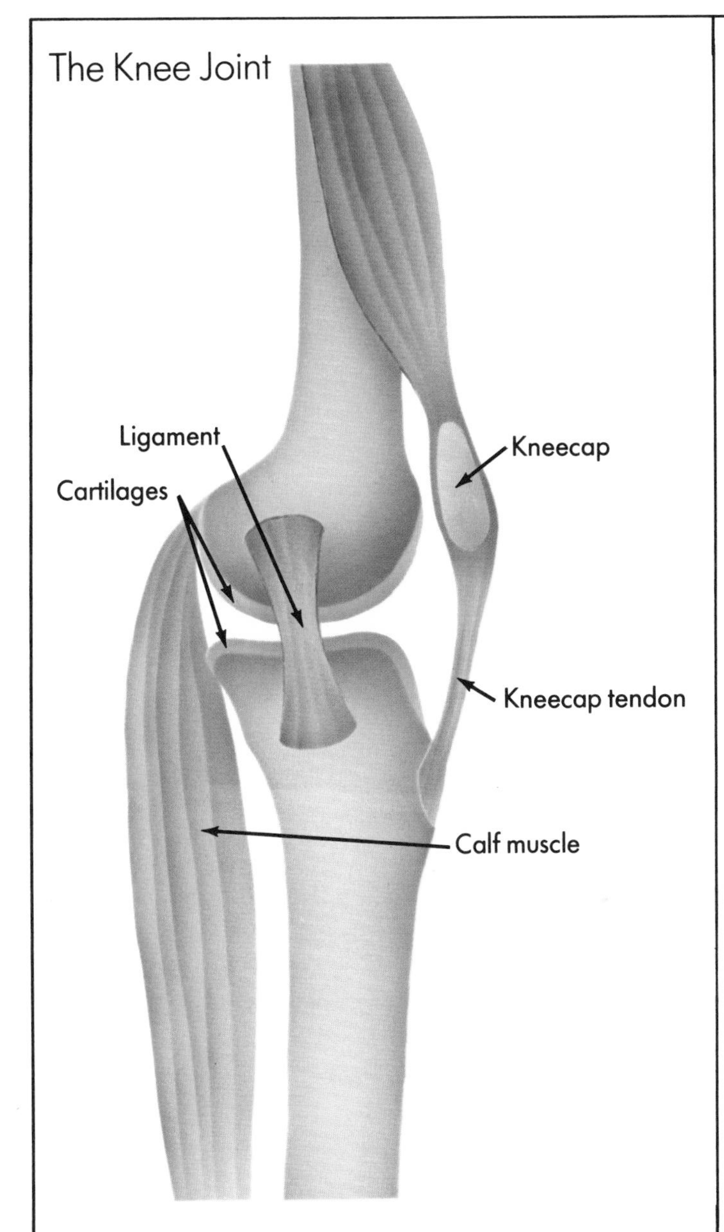

Dislocations are a serious joint injury. A joint is dislocated whenever the bones which compose it are pulled out of their normal position. This occurs when a person's arm, finger, shoulder, or leg is forced out of place by a fall, pull, or blow. Often ligaments and tendons are injured when a dislocation occurs. Dislocations are normally accompanied by intense pain, tenderness, and swelling at or near the joint. Abnormal appearance and loss of movement may also occur.

You should immediately support the injured part in the most comfortable position, using padding and bandages or slings. Cold compresses may reduce swelling. Call for medical help as soon as you have administered first aid.

A severe blow to the joints can break or chip the cartilage. Cartilage can also be damaged by the continuous wearing down of one cartilage rubbing against another. This injury happens most often in the knee joint; it requires consultation with a doctor and possible hospitalization.

When ligaments are stretched or torn, the injury is called a **sprain**. The most common sprains occur in the ankle or knee; however, they may also happen to the finger, knee, thumb, hip, or wrist. Sprains usually result from a blow, twisting or turning over of a joint. Swelling, pain, and discoloration of the skin are common signs of this injury. When a sprain occurs, stop exercising and apply ice, compression, and elevation. If the pain is severe, you should see a doctor as there may be a cracked or broken bone.

I.C.E.

In general, where injuries to muscles and joints are involved (sprains, strains, and bruises), the first-aid treatment should be I.C.E.—an abbreviation for the procedure explained below:

Ice: Applying ice decreases the bleeding from injured blood vessels and minimizes swelling if applied for 5 to 15 min. Repeat every 2.5 h for one to two days.

Compression: Compression also limits swelling which, if uncontrolled, could delay healing. Compression can be accomplished by wrapping the injured joint or putting a boot on if the injury is at the ankle.

Elevation: Raising the injured part to above the level of the heart uses gravity to help drain excess fluid and keep swelling down.

Because swelling usually starts within seconds of an injury, start I.C.E. as soon as possible.

Head, Neck, and Face Injuries

Although these injuries do not occur as often as others, they can be very severe when they do happen. Sometimes they result in paralysis or even death.

Concussion is a common head injury which may happen when the head is hit or jarred. A person who has suffered concussion may experience double vision and headaches. If these signs persist or if the person becomes unusually sleepy, keep him or her awake and consult a doctor immediately.

Head injuries can be prevented by wearing a good helmet. Even small children learning to ice-skate are now wearing them. They are common in sports such as baseball, football, horseback riding, lacrosse, skiing, hockey, motorcycle and auto racing, skateboarding, and white water canoeing.

The face is a part of the body very open to injury. The eyes, nose, and mouth are commonly hurt. These injuries can be particularly serious because the damage done may be permanent and disfiguring.

There is evidence that wearing face protectors dramatically reduces the chance of injury. For example, statistics show that 75% fewer Canadian amateur hockey players were blinded in the 1975-76 season than in the previous year. Much of this reduction in injury was a direct result of the wide use of face masks. Studies have also shown that the wearing of both faceguard and mouth protection ensures practically 100% protection against oral injury.

People are now much more conscious of safety than they were in the past. Protective glasses especially designed for certain sports have become standard equipment. "Combat glasses" are worn by players in activities such as squash, racquetball, hockey, football, basketball, and swimming. The plastic wrap-around lens and frame provide protection to the eye and temple. Glasses are available in plain or prescriptive models.

THE HELMET

Helmets work by absorbing the impact of a blow. Next to the shell are packs of stiff foam which act as shock absorbers. However, in order to give maximum protection, a helmet must fit properly. A correctly fitted helmet will protect the entire skull, and, in particular, the forehead, the temples, the ear area, and the base of the skull. The forehead should be covered so that no more than the width of one finger will fit between the helmet and the eyebrows. To ensure effective protection, it is important also to fasten the chin strap.

Proper equipment will ensure a safer game.

FIRST-AID PROCEDURES

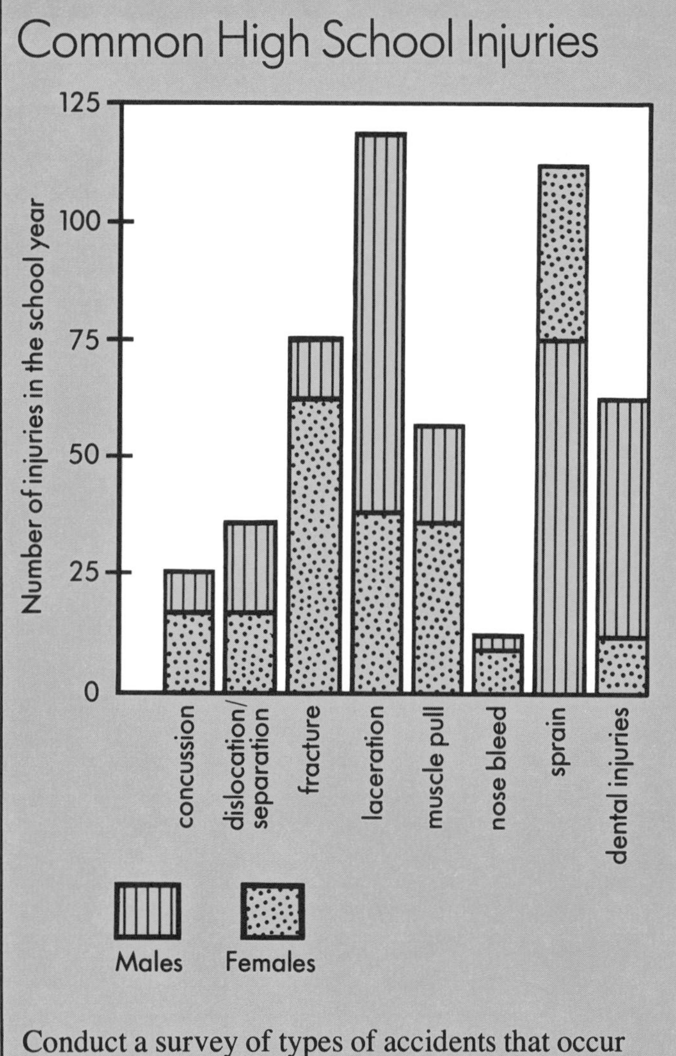

Conduct a survey of types of accidents that occur in your school. Keep separate totals for girls and boys. Which is the most common injury for males and which for females? Suggest some reasons for the difference.

In order to be prepared for serious injuries you should have some knowledge of first aid. Detailed courses of study are available from your local St. John Ambulance Association and the Canadian Red Cross Association. Consequently the remainder of this chapter will only cover the most basic aspects of this important topic.

As the initial step in first aid, you should check the three "B's". In order of importance, these are: (1) breathing (2) bleeding (3) broken bones. The order is significant because if you come upon a person requiring help, you should discover and treat lack of breathing first, bleeding second, and broken bones third. A knowledge of the treatment for **shock** is also important in basic first aid.

Breathing

If you see a person who is conscious but unable to breathe, you must first clear away the obstruction in the air passage. If the obstacles cannot be seen and removed by the finger, the following procedure should be followed:

1. Take up a position behind the victim.
2. Deliver four sharp blows between the shoulder blades of the person.
3. Place fist around person, thumb side against person's abdomen above navel and below breastbone.
4. Place your other open hand over your fist.

5. With a quick upward thrust, press forcefully into abdomen four times.
6. If object is not ejected, repeat processes 2, 3, 4, and 5.

CAUTION: If you practise this technique on someone who is not choking, be sure to press gently so that he or she is not injured.

Removing an obstruction when the person is conscious.

If you are the person choking and you are alone or not helped immediately in the manner just described, try to duplicate the procedure on yourself as follows:

1. Clasp your hands as shown in the following diagram below.
2. Press down forcefully on your "double fist" by bending over the back of a chair, desk, table, or other solid surface.

A trial practice of this technique will make you much better prepared should you ever choke.

Removing an obstruction when you are choking.

A person may also be unconscious with a blocked airway. The position of the tongue is the major cause of obstructed breathing. Tilting the head so that the chin points up will open the airway. The obstruction may be something else such as regurgitated food, water, a small object, or a piece of food in the windpipe. In order to remove this kind of obstruction, you should proceed as follows:

1. Place the victim on his or her back.
2. Facing the victim, kneel astride the hips.
3. With one of your hands on top of the other, place the heel of your bottom hand on the abdomen slightly above the navel and below the rib cage.
4. Press forcefully into the abdomen with a quick upward thrust. Turn the person onto the side and try to remove the obstruction with your fingers.
5. Repeat several times if necessary.

Removing an obstruction when the person is unconscious.

If the object (food, water in lungs, toy) has been expelled, or removed by your fingers and the person does not resume breathing, you must immediately begin **artificial respiration**:

1. Tilt the head so that the chin points up.
2. Place your mouth tightly over the person's mouth and close the nostrils with your fingers.
3. Blow into the mouth until the chest rises.
4. Remove mouth and release nostrils. Listen for the sound of air escaping from the lungs.
5. Repeat the above every 5 s for adults and every 3 s for children.
6. Keep at it until the person breathes.
7. Get medical help.

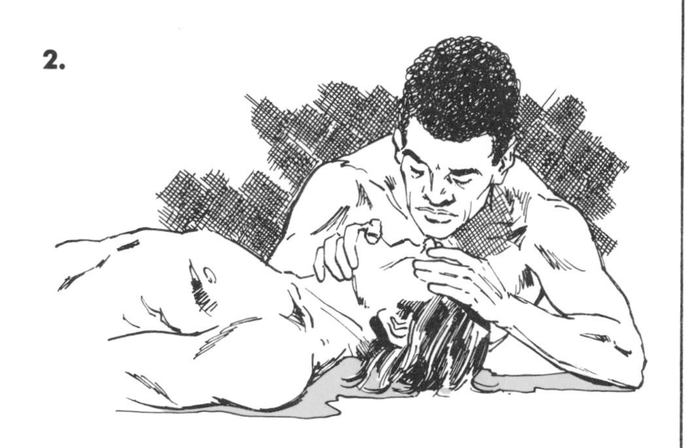

Artificial respiration

Bleeding

The human body contains approximately 5 L of blood. Severe loss of this supply can be fatal. It is important to get the person to a hospital as soon as possible. To help a person who is bleeding heavily, do the following: cover the wound immediately with the cleanest cloth available or with your bare hand, control bleeding by direct pressure on the wound, and elevate the injured area unless there is a broken bone or an embedded object.

If the bleeding is minor, wash out the wound with water and wipe or swab any dirt away from the cut. If bleeding persists, apply firm pressure to the bleeding points. Finally, dress the wound with a sterile bandage, tape firmly, and keep the bleeding part elevated. Remember that if the wound is difficult to clean, the person may need a tetanus shot. Check with a doctor.

If the bleeding is from the nose, there is a special first-aid technique that you can use. First, seat the victim with the head bent slightly forward and loosen the clothing around the neck. Pinch the front part of the nostrils for about 10 min while applying cold compresses to the forehead and the back of the neck. If the bleeding persists or recurs, it may be a sign of a more severe medical problem. In this case, it is important to seek medical help.

Treating Broken Bones

You should suspect a broken bone or fracture if there is pain when the victim moves the injured part, if there is swelling and tenderness in the area, or if there is deformity of the bones.

The first-aid procedure for fractures is as follows:

1. Do not move the victim unless he or she is in the path of immediate danger. Back or neck injuries may be present.
2. Place the limb in as normal a position as possible without causing excessive pain.
3. Apply an emergency splint to support the injured part in one position, reduce pain, and prevent further injury.

Be sure to seek medical help as soon as you have administered first aid.

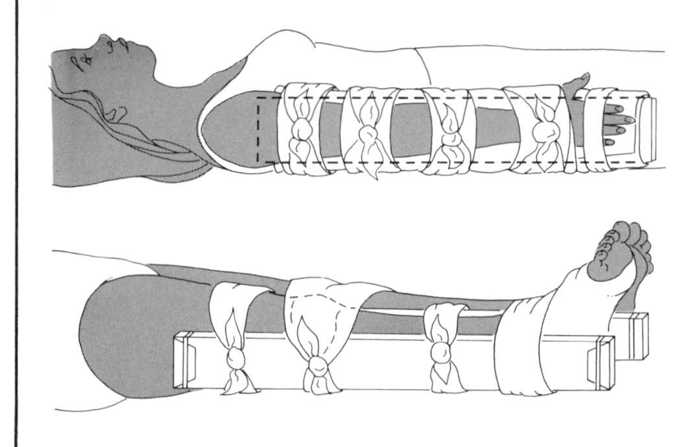

Shock

Shock is the acute failure of the circulation of blood to the body. In every case of injury there is some shock and, if the shock is severe and untreated, it can lead to death. Shock can also be caused by excessive heat, illness, or sudden stress.

You can usually tell when a person is in shock by a pale face, perspiration, possible dizziness, and nausea. When a person appears to be in shock, you should proceed as follows:

1. Call for medical aid.
2. Place the head level or lower than the feet (unless injury would be aggravated by this position).
3. Loosen tight clothing.
4. Keep the person warm to maintain normal body temperature.
5. Reassure the person.
6. Give the person fluids (not alcohol), if not unconscious, nauseated, or severely wounded in the abdomen.

Fainting results from an inadequate supply of blood to the brain. If this occurs, proceed with the above steps for treatment of shock. Gradually raise the person to a sitting position as consciousness returns and give sips of water if required.

Heat exhaustion produces symptoms much like shock, due to heat retention in the body. Dizziness, muscle cramps, weak pulse, and cold clammy skin are signs that a person is suffering from excessive heat. If these symptoms are present, place the person in a cool area and provide a drink of cold water. If the person is unconscious, do not give anything by mouth, but seek medical help.

WHAT WOULD YOU DO?

You are walking near a small lake in an isolated part of the country. As you approach the lake, you hear a person choking in desperation. You hurry to the spot where the sound came from to find a boy lying on his stomach with his arm bent under him in a very unnatural position. He has a deep gash on his leg that is bleeding slowly. When you speak to him, there is no response. List in order of importance what you would do.

SAFETY — A LIFETIME HABIT

Injuries due to activity can generally be avoided by common sense and a knowledge of safeguards. If injuries do occur, steps can be taken to inhibit further aggravation and serious complications. Finally, if the injury is serious, an understanding of first aid may prevent severe damage and even death. Your knowledge and the ability to apply this knowledge could be very important.

FOR REVIEW

Key Ideas

- General rules for athletic activity include: choosing the proper clothing and equipment for the activity; not continuing an activity if you experience pain; always including a warm-up before the activity and a cool-down afterward.
- Common injuries can be prevented and, if they occur, easily treated.
- Most serious injuries that occur during physical activity involve bones, joints, head, neck, and the face.
- A knowledge of first aid will prepare you to deal with serious injuries.

Questions and Activities

1. Explain why a warm-up and a cool-down are important aspects of physical activity.
2. Describe briefly how the following injuries can be prevented and how they should be treated: blister, athlete's foot, muscle cramp, and tendonitis.
3. How does concussion occur and how should it be treated?
4. What basic signs should you check first when you are giving first aid?
5. Survey a school team on injuries that have occurred during the school year. The coach or manager might be the best person to answer the following questionnaire:
   a. How many injuries have occurred during the school year?
   b. How many of these were serious (involving the head, face or bones)?
   c. Were any of these sports injuries preventable? How?
6. Interview your school team coach about the pre-season and pre-game conditioning exercises.
7. Find out about Cardiopulmonary Resuscitation courses in your area. Report on the requirements to complete the course and other possible benefits you could obtain from getting your Basic Rescuer certificate.
8. Describe any personal injuries you or your family may have had over the past five years, what you did about them, and whether you could have prevented the injuries.
9. Find out the names of approved helmets for one of the following sports:
   a. hockey
   b. skateboarding
   c. football
   d. baseball.

CHAPTER FOUR

FOOD AND WHAT IT DOES FOR YOU

NUTRITION IN ADOLESCENCE

Good nutrition is especially important at this time of your life because many changes are taking place in your body. Your bones are becoming longer, your muscles are larger and stronger, and your body is producing more fat. Because you have entered a period of rapid growth and development, there are a number of nutrients that are essential to your health. Calcium is needed for healthy bones and teeth. Iron for the body tissues and blood production is also important, especially for girls who have started their menstrual cycle. Extra proteins are necessary because of your new growth in height, mass, and muscle structure.

While all of the foods necessary for proper nutrition are readily available, a Nutrition Canada survey has shown that the diet of many adolescents is deficient. The survey noted, in particular, a shortage of calcium, iron, and vitamin D. In order to ensure good health as you grow, you should eat a variety of foods each day from the four food groups. Variety is important because no single food contains all of the nutrients in the quantities needed by the body.

Milk and Milk Products

3–4 servings daily
1 serving = 250 mL milk, 125 mL yogurt or cottage cheese
= 45 g hard or processed cheese

Meat and Alternates

2 servings daily
1 serving = 90 g cooked lean meat, poultry, liver, or fish
= 60 mL peanut butter
= 125 mL nuts or seeds
= 60 g hard, process, or cottage cheese
= 2 eggs

Bread and Cereals

3–5 servings daily, whole-grain or enriched bread and whole-grain cereal recommended
1 serving= 1 roll, 1 muffin, or 1 slice of bread
= 200 mL cooked or ready-to-eat cereal
= 250 mL cooked rice or pasta

Fruits and Vegetables

4–5 servings daily including at least 2 vegetables
1 serving= 125 mL vegetables or fruits
= 125 mL juice
=1 medium potato, carrot, tomato, peach, apple, orange, or banana

Do you frequently skip breakfast? It may be tempting to do without it or settle for a cup of coffee if you are in a hurry. Some dieters mistakenly think they can reduce their body mass this way. However, if you go without this important meal you will find yourself hungry

KNOW THE NUTRIENTS

during the day when you may not be able to eat nutritious food. If you do not eat until lunchtime you will be going up to 18 h without food. Starting with a good meal will ensure that you have lots of energy throughout the day. A satisfactory breakfast should include at least three of the food groups.

Snacks can be nutritious if you select the right foods. However, they should not be substitutes for meals. Snacks which will satisfy your appetite and offer you good nutrition include nuts, fruit, whole grain bread, crackers and cheese, and yogurt. Cakes, cookies, doughnuts, candy, soft drinks, and potato chips are examples of snacks that should be avoided. They are high in food energy but contain few nutrients. Sweet snacks also stick to your teeth, encouraging the development of cavities.

Try these snacks.

Most authorities agree that the six basic elements in a nutritious diet are carbohydrates, fats and oils, proteins, minerals, vitamins, and water. Fibre is another important ingredient. You should know how a proper balance of these nutrients contributes to your good health, in particular, to your energy level. Food energy is measured in units known as kilojoules.

Carbohydrates

Carbohydrates, the sugars and starches in foods, are the main supply of energy for the body. They contribute 45% – 50% of your total energy intake. The major sources of carbohydrates are sweet fruits, cereal grains, and plant roots. Fruits contain carbohydrates in the form of sugar while grains and root vegetables contain carbohydrates in the form of starch.

When you eat a food containing carbohydrates, your digestive system breaks down the sugar and starch into simple sugars which act as fuel for the body. The most essential form of sugar for body energy is called **glucose** or "blood sugar".

Some foods containing carbohydrates are better for you than others. Fruits such as apples, oranges, and bananas, and root vegetables such as potatoes, carrots, and beets are recommended because they also contain vitamins and minerals. The grains or cereal plants such as wheat, rice, and corn in their natural state are rich in vitamins

The Food Groups
yogurt
Milk and Milk Products
Peanut Butter
Meat and Alternatives
New
Cereal
Bread and Cereals
Fruits and Vegetables

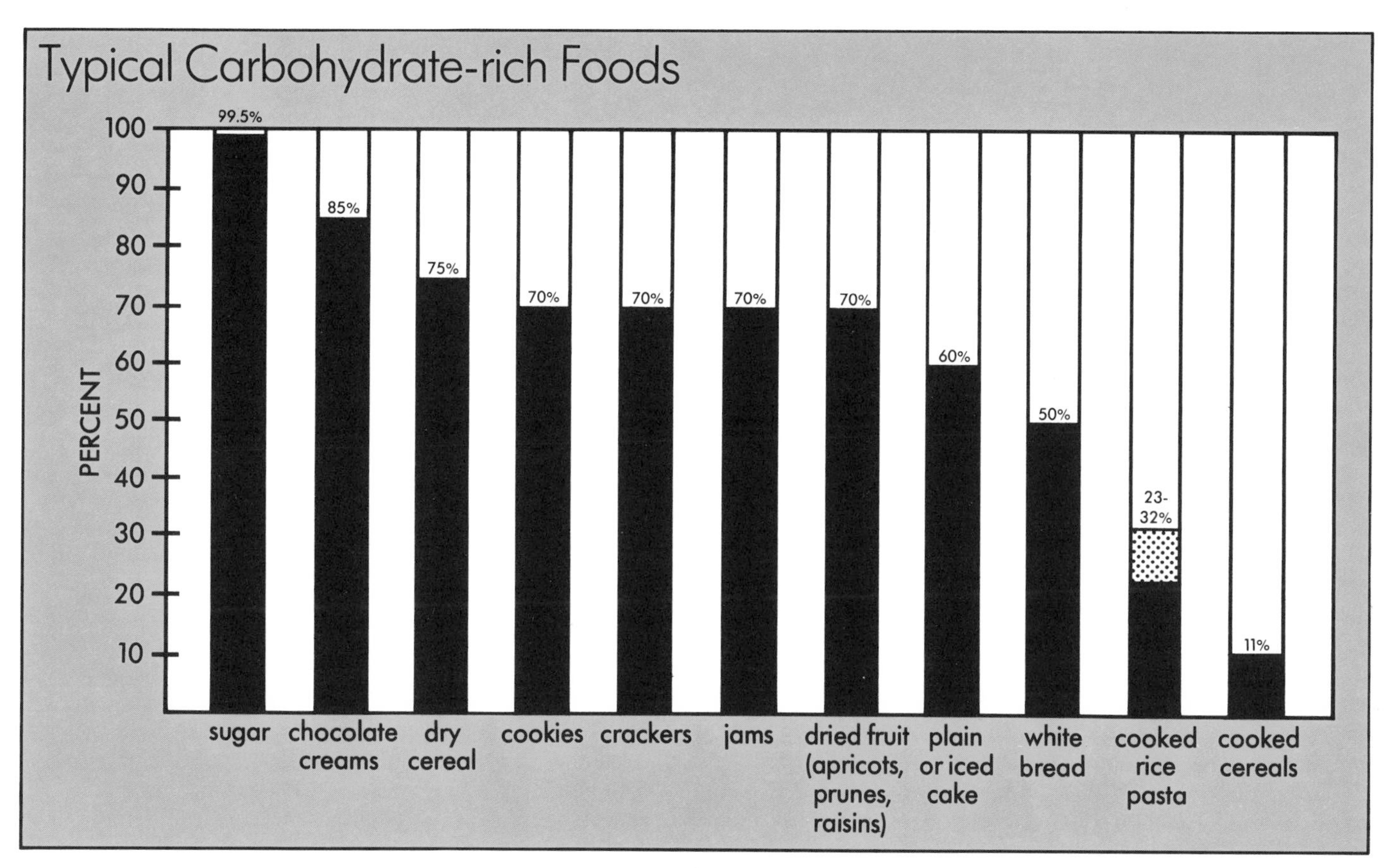

and minerals as well. Unfortunately, people today tend to rely on foods that are not particularly good sources of carbohydrates. During food processing, nutrients are often removed and extra sugar is added. This sugar is sometimes called hidden sugar. People also add sugar to foods in various forms: white sugar, brown sugar, honey, or molasses. Although honey and molasses offer some nutritional value, white sugar and brown sugar have none.

In North America, about 25% of most people's needed food energy comes from extra sugar. Canadians average 45 kg per year (125 g per day). This places a tremendous burden on the other foods people eat to supply the needed nutrients. Sugar has also been implicated in tooth decay. It is recommended that people reduce their refined sugar intake from 25% of their total food energy to 15%.

Hidden Sugars in Food*

Food	Portion	Sugar (in g)	Food	Portion	Sugar (in g)
Soft drinks	250 mL	25	Pie	1 slice	35-50
Cake, plain	125 g	15	Pastry	1 piece	15
Cake, iced	125 g	50	Tart	1	40
Cookie	1	10	Pudding	125 mL	15
Doughnut, plain	1	10	Flavoured Gelatin	125 mL	25
Doughnut, iced	1	30	Brown sugar	25 mL	15
Chocolate bar	1 small	40	White sugar	25 mL	15
Chewing gum	1 piece	2	Honey	25 mL	15
Hard candy	125 g	100	Maple syrup	25 mL	20
Canned fruit	250 mL	50-100	White bread	1 slice	2
Canned fruit juice	125 mL	10	Hot Dog Bun	1 bun	5
Ice cream	1 scoop	20	Cereal	200 mL (+ 5 mL Sugar)	20-40
Sundae	1	35	Ketchup	25 mL	5
Chocolate milk	1 glass	10	Jam	25 mL	20
Milk shake	300 mL	25	Peanut Butter	125 mL	8

*An average quantity of sugar is listed.

Activities

1. Using the above chart calculate the amount of sugar contained in a soft drink, a hamburger with ketchup, a milk shake and a glazed doughnut. You may want to actually measure the amount of sugar by putting it on a scale.
2. Calculate the total amount of sugar in the following foods: 200 mL of cereal, 1 piece of iced cake, 125 g of hard candy, a glass of chocolate milk, and 250 mL of flavoured gelatin.

NUTRITION AND ATHLETIC ACTIVITY

If you are athletically active, you will have special nutritional needs. Here are a few pointers concerning nutrition and athletic activity.

1. Exercise requires more energy than non-activity. Therefore, it is important to consume high energy nutrients. A balanced diet with some additional carbohydrates will provide the extra energy. Eating more protein was at one time thought to be beneficial, but this theory is no longer held.
2. The food you eat before a game should be enjoyable and easily digestible. This means you should avoid eating foods such as the traditional steak dinner that are high in fats. You may want to include a small quantity of sugar for extra energy. A good pre-game meal might include fruit punch, sandwiches, and ice milk.
3. You need extra fluid when you train or compete. In addition to sweating, you eliminate water with each breath. Drink extra fluid before performing.
4. You should not train or perform on a full stomach. Wait at least 1 h, preferably 2 h, before strenuous exercise.
5. Because of emotional stress, it takes 2 to 4 h longer for the stomach to empty on game days than on non-game days. Make sure you finish eating well ahead of an activity.

I wonder if this is good for me.

Fats

Fats produce the most energy per gram of any food. About 40% of your food energy comes from fats. Ideally, this should be reduced to about 35%. Some fat is obviously necessary for the body. It is used as insulation against heat and cold. It also protects the body organs against injury.

There are two types of fats. **Saturated fat** is found in animal products such as beef, eggs, cheese, and butter. **Unsaturated fats** are found in vegetables such as corn and peanut oil, and in certain types of margarine. **Polyunsaturated fat**,

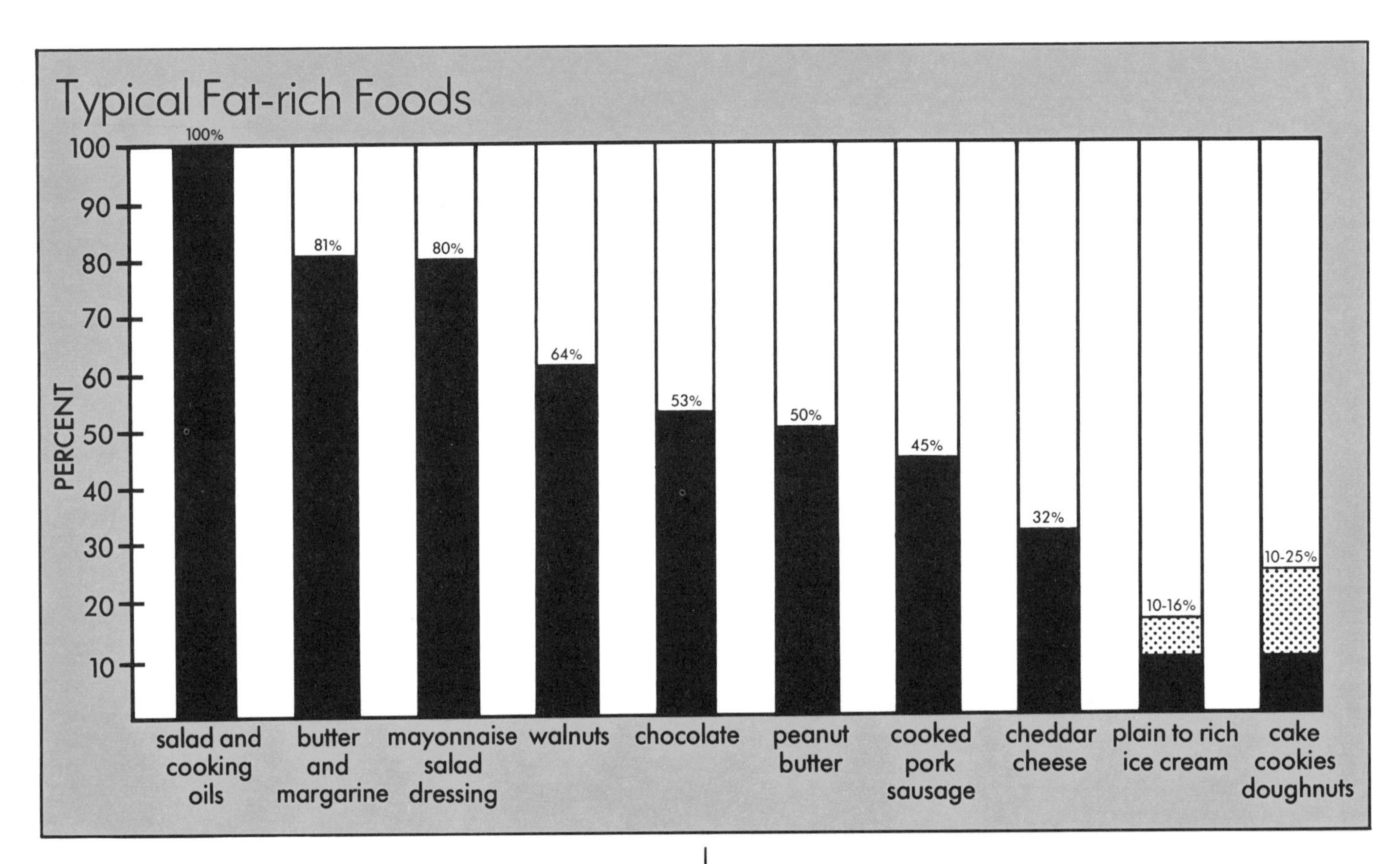

a type of unsaturated fat, is found in some seeds and nuts.

There is some controversy about the effects of saturated fats, which contain cholesterol, on the health of the body. As you read in the chapter on cardiorespiratory fitness, there may be an association between cholesterol and heart and blood vessel disease. Since the effect of saturated fats in the diet is still being researched, a balanced diet of saturated and unsaturated fats is recommended.

Proteins

Proteins are important in the body because, next to water, they make up most of the skin, tendons, muscle, and other body tissues. They are essential for repairing and maintaining body cells and are necessary for growth. Proteins also supply additional energy.

Proteins are complex substances. They are formed from twenty-two different **amino acids**.

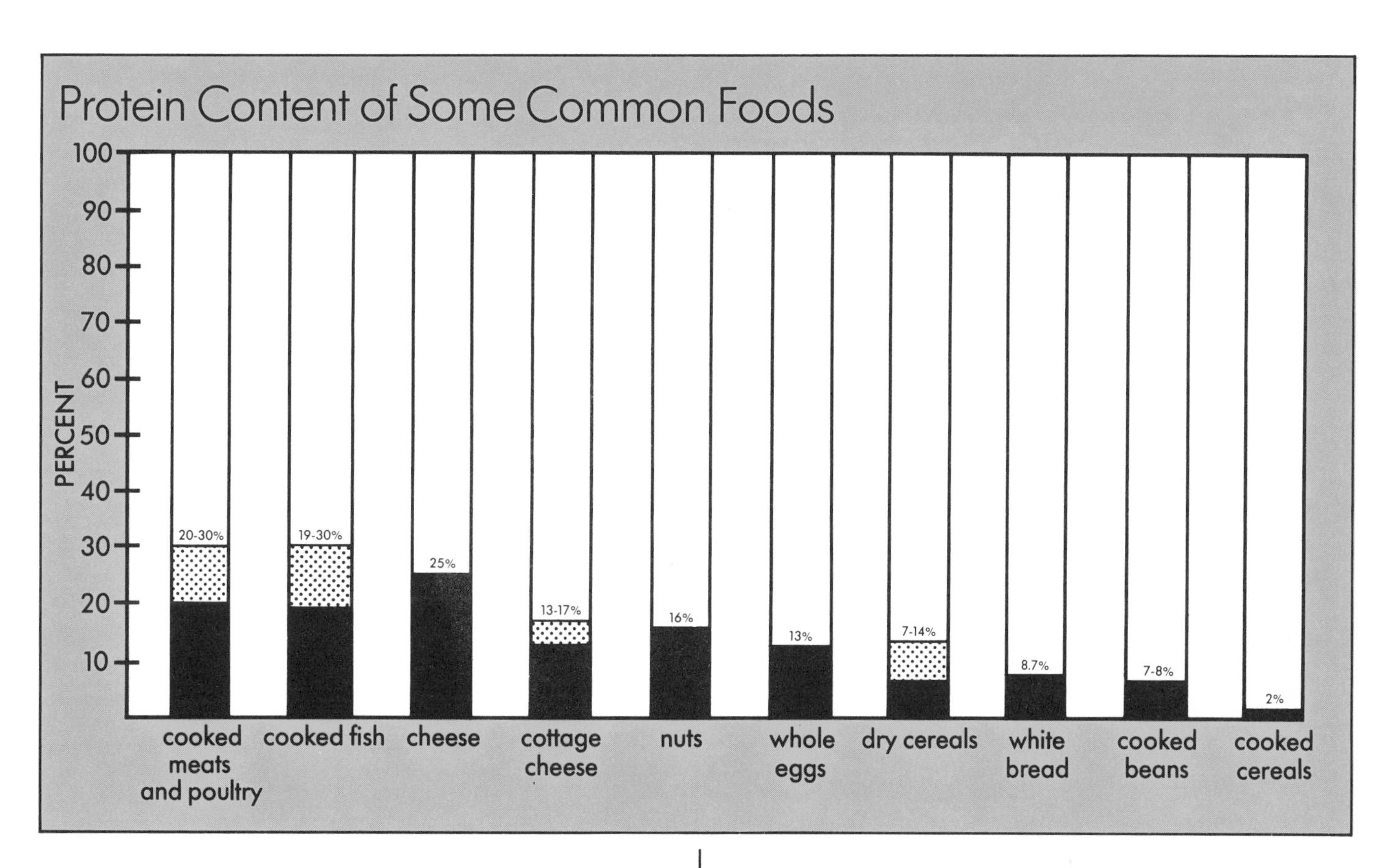

Your body produces about half the amino acids it needs for making body tissue. However, it cannot make nine of the amino acids. They are called essential amino acids because they must come from food sources alone.

If a food provides all of the essential amino acids that the body needs, it is said to contain a complete protein. Meat, fish, eggs, cheese, and milk all supply a complete protein. These foods come from animals that have already manufactured the essential amino acids. Most vegetables contain an incomplete protein, that is, they cannot provide all of the essential amino acids. People who follow only a vegetarian diet, then, must generally eat a variety of vegetables in order to obtain a complete protein.

VEGETARIAN DIETS

Foods of vegetable origin which contain protein are nuts, seeds (sunflower, sesame), legumes (peas, beans) and grains (wheat, oats, rice). Most of these plants have an incomplete protein. However, certain plant combinations and plant foods eaten with milk products will give a complete protein. It is important that these food combinations be eaten at the same meal so that complete protein is obtained.

People eating only plant foods should also make certain to obtain the vitamins and minerals found most abundantly in animal products. These include vitamin B^{12}, vitamin D, and iron. Many vegetarians eat cheese and eggs and drink milk to ensure that they receive all of the necessary nutrients. Vegetarians who include dairy products and eggs in their diets are called lacto-ovo-vegetarians.

Vegetarian diets have been followed for centuries, sometimes because religious or moral beliefs dictated this and sometimes because meat has been scarce. Such a diet can be beneficial if care is taken to include all of the nutrients needed for health. For example, a study of Seventh Day Adventists (who are vegetarians) showed that the incidence of cancer of the colon was much lower among this group than in the general population.

Minerals

Minerals are needed in the body for a variety of purposes. They do not function alone but in association with other nutrients in the body. They keep the skeletal system strong and help in the formation of red blood cells as well as protect the teeth against decay. There are at least sixteen minerals needed for good health. Most of these are readily available through a balanced diet. However, you should make a point to choose foods containing calcium and iron, because these minerals are especially important when your body is growing. Fluorine is added to drinking water and iodine is obtained by using iodized salt, or by eating seafood. You will get enough phosphorus if you eat foods rich in calcium. The other eleven minerals are easily obtained by eating a variety of foods.

Eaten in the proper proportions, vegetarian foods will give you complete protein.

Minerals

Mineral	Functions	Important Sources
Calcium	Necessary for: 1. Strong bones and sound teeth. 2. Maintenance and response of nerves and muscles, i.e. muscle tone. 3. Normal clotting of blood. 4. Prevention of rickets. 5. Normal regulation of heartbeat.	Milk, Cheese, Canned salmon and sardines (with bones), Shellfish, Egg yolk, Broccoli, Dried beans, Turnip greens, Beet greens, Soy beans.
Phosphorus	Necessary for: 1. Strong bones and sound teeth. 2. Metabolism of proteins, fats and carbohydrates. 3. Formation and function of all body cells. 4. Buffer action in blood and muscles.	Meat, Poultry, Fish, Eggs, Yeast, Milk, Cheese, Nuts, Legumes (beans, peas).
Iron	Necessary for: 1. Formation of hemoglobin and red blood cells. 2. Tissue respiration and transport of oxygen. 3. Prevention of simple anemia.	Liver, Heart, Kidney, Lean meat, Egg yolk, Shellfish, Yeast, Dried beans and other legumes, Dried fruits, Molasses and brown sugar.
Copper	Necessary for: 1. Formation of hemoglobin and red blood cells. 2. Prevention of anemia of infancy.	Liver, Dried peas and beans, Whole grain cereals or bread, Chocolate, Mushrooms, Eggs.
Iodine	Necessary for: 1. Formation of thyroxin, the hormone of the thryoid gland. Thyroxin regulates the rate of metabolic functions. 2. Prevention of simple goiter.	Sea foods, Iodized salt, Fruits and vegetables produced on soils of good iodine content.

Water-soluble Vitamins

Vitamin	Functions	Important Sources
Vitamin B_1 - Thiamine	Necessary for: 1. Growth. 2. Pregnancy and lactation. 3. Maintenance of good appetite and normal digestion. 4. Normal functioning of nervous system. 5. Metabolism of carbohydrates. 6. Prevention of beri-beri.	Pork, Organ meats (liver, heart, kidney) Lean meat, Beans, Peas, Egg yolk, Spinach, Asparagus, Nuts, Whole grain cereals and breads, Milk, Potatoes
Vitamin B_2 - Riboflavin	Necessary for: 1. Growth and reproduction. 2. Maximal life span. 3. Normal activities of cells. 4. Normal functioning of nervous system. 5. Normal healthy condition of skin and eyes.	Organ meats (liver, kidney, heart), Milk, Cheese, Meat, Eggs, Green leafy vegetables
Nicotinic-Acid - Niacin Nicotinamide, Niacinamide	Necessary for: 1. Growth. 2. Metabolism. 3. Prevention of pellagra. 4. Maintenance of normal function of gastro-intestinal tract. 5. Maintenance of skin condition.	Liver, Meat, Whole grain cereals and bread, Fish, Dried peas and beans, Nuts and peanut butter
Vitamin C - Ascorbic acid, Cevitamic acid	Necessary for: 1. Growth. 2. Prevention of scurvy. 3. Sound teeth, gums, and bones. 4. Maintenance of normal strength of capillary walls. 5. Metabolism of certain amino acids. 6. Resistance to infections.	Citrus fruits and juices (orange, grapefruit and lemons), Tomatoes, Potatoes, Liver, Cantaloupe, Strawberries, Spinach, Brussel sprouts, Broccoli, Cauliflower, Parsley, Green peppers, Radishes

Fat-soluble Vitamins

Vitamin	Functions	Important Sources
Vitamin A - Carotenes	Necessary for: 1. Growth of bones and teeth. 2. Maintaining normal resistance to infection. 3. Pregnancy and lactation. 4. Adjusting the eye to different intensities of light.	Liver, Egg yolk, Fish liver oils, Dark green leafy and deep yellow vegetables, Apricots, Cantaloupe, Tomatoes and tomato products, Butter, Fortified margarine, Cream and cheese.
Vitamin D - Calciferol, Activiated 7-dehydrocholesterol, etc.	Necessary for: 1. Sound teeth and strong bones. 2. Regulation of calcium and phosphorus metabolism. 3. Prevention of rickets.	Fish liver oils, Liver, Egg yolks, Salt-water fish, Foods fortified with vitamin D—such as evaporated milk, Direct sunlight (produces D in the skin of exposed person).
Vitamin K - Naphtoquinones, Menadione	Necessary for: 1. Normal clotting of blood.	Spinach, Cauliflower, Cabbage, Soy beans, Pork liver, Oats, Wheat bran

Vitamins

Vitamins are an essential part of a proper diet since they are needed for healthy tissues, bones, and blood. Vitamins are usually divided into two categories. Water-soluble vitamins (B and C) are found in the watery parts of cells and in foods such as fruits which contain a high percentage of water. They are used by the body in a short time or flushed out in the urine. It is important to maintain a balanced diet so that water-soluble vitamins are always present in the body. Fat-

THE VITAMIN C CONTROVERSY

The recommended daily allowance for vitamin C is 45 mg or a small glass of orange juice. Most people take more than required in the foods they eat in one day. There is controversy over whether vitamin C in large doses has any effect on stress, the common cold or other diseases.

soluble vitamins (A, D, E, and K) are dissolved and stored in the fat part of the body cells. If large quantities of these vitamins are taken, they can accumulate in the cells and may cause damage. A balanced diet will provide all of the vitamins necessary for health.

Water

40–60% of total body mass is made up of water. It is needed for all chemical reactions in the body and acts as a lubricant for digestion, excretion, and circulation. Water is part of saliva, blood, and other body fluids.

Each day you lose about 2.5 L of water through sweat, urine, and respiration. In summer you keep cool by evaporation of water in the lungs and by sweating. You replace this water loss through beverages or food containing water. Even at rest, with moderate temperatures, an adult can only stay alive for about a week without water, compared to five weeks without food.

Most people obtain their water through various beverages. What you drink can make a difference to your health. For example, tea, coffee, cocoa, and some soft drinks contain **caffeine**. This drug, if taken in excess, can cause restlessness, headaches, and irritability, and may even interfere with your sleep. Soft drinks supply only non-nutritional energy as do sugar-sweetened "fruit drinks" (unless they have added vitamin C). The best beverages for your health are natural fruit and vegetable juices, water, and milk.

FACTS ABOUT CAFFEINE

Caffeine is found in coffee, tea and cola. The amount of caffeine in coffee varies from 150 to 700 mg/L, depending on strength, amount and type of coffee (freeze dried is much lower than percolated or drip coffee). Tea averages about 180 mg/L and a 350 mL can of cola drink contains approximately 35 mg of caffeine. It has been shown that a regular intake of 350 mg per day can cause physical dependence. If caffeine consumption is reduced or stopped, withdrawal symptoms of fatigue, headache, and irritability can occur.

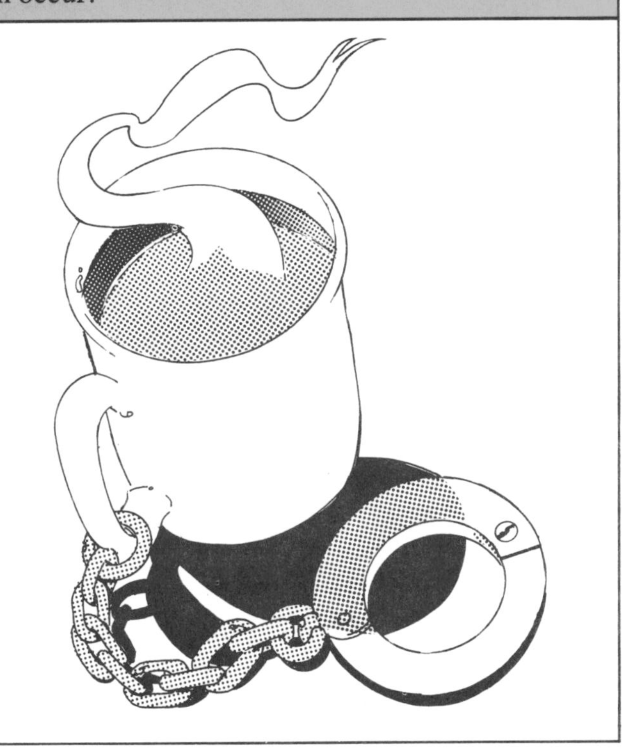

KNOW WHAT YOU EAT

Fibre

Although vegetable fibre is not actually a nutrient, it is important in your diet. It is contained in whole grains, peas, beans, fruits, and vegetables. Fibre cannot be absorbed by your body but it helps your large intestine work more efficiently to eliminate food wastes. Because many of the foods people eat today contain little fibre, the process of elimination becomes less efficient. Therefore, try to include as many unrefined foods as possible in your diet.

Since most of the foods you eat have been bought in stores, you do not have a lot of control over what happens to them before you get them. In some cases, you certainly benefit; in other cases, you may actually be harmed.

Today many foods are processed. This means that these foods have been changed somehow from their original state. In some cases, processing is very simple. Dirt, for example is usually washed off fresh vegetables. In other cases, processing is very complex. It can involve crushing, heating, pickling, freezing, whipping, and adding chemicals.

Modern processing methods have made it possible for consumers to buy an immense variety of attractive foods whenever they wish.

MYSTERY FOODS

The following ingredients are listed on two food packages. Can you identify each food?

a. sugar, dextrose, citric acid, natural lemon flavour (contains BHA—a preservative) trisodium citrate, tricalcium phosphate, gum arabic, vitamin C (214 mg/100 g), vegetable shortening, food colour.

(*fruit drink crystals*)

b. enriched flour, potato flour, lard (and may contain vegetable oil, beef tallow, palm oil), hydrogenated vegetable oil (and may contain coconut oil), cheddar cheese, milk solids, sour cream solids, whey powder, salt, sugar (and may contain dextrose), ammonium bicarbonate, sodium bicarbonate, calcium acid phosphate, sodium stearoyl—2 lactylate, hydrolized plant protein, chives, parsley, spices, monosodium glutamate, gum arabic, lactic acid, acetic acid, artificial colour and flavour, protease.

(*cheese flavoured crackers*)

Try asking your friends to identify a food by its list of ingredients.

Modern processing methods have made it possible for consumers to buy an immense variety of attractive foods whenever they wish. Freezing and canning methods mean that all year round you can have the benefit of fruits and vegetables you would otherwise eat only when they came into season. Because of processing, there are also many foods available that you can eat with little or no prepartion (T.V. dinners, frozen pizza). Preservatives added to foods like bread and meat ensure that they keep their freshness longer than a day or two. Other additives are used to make food more attractive and, therefore, more pleasant to eat. These additives affect flavour, texture, and colour. For example, artificial lemon flavouring is added to fruit drinks and pie fillings, and artificial smoke flavouring is added to bacon and nuts. Red dye is used in wieners and maraschino cherries to improve colour.

While food processing gives the consumer a wide variety of foods to choose from, scientists are becoming aware of loss of nutritional value and potential health hazards. White bread, for example, is made from wheat flour that has had the bran and the wheat germ removed. Bran is a good source of fibre which aids the body in eliminating wastes. The wheat germ contains the vast majority of the vitamins and minerals in wheat. To compensate for this loss, some vitamins are put back into the flour. When you see the terms "enriched" bread or "enriched" flour, you know it has added vitamins. However, not all of the vitamins and minerals which have been removed have been put back and none of the bran has been put back. Thus, whole-wheat bread is a much better choice than white bread.

There is considerable concern that some additives are potential health hazards. Most smoked meats have chemicals added to them to extend the length of time they are safe to eat. The two main chemicals found in fried bacon (sodium nitrate and sodium nitrite) have been linked to cancer. Food colouring (or dye) is used in almost all packaged foods, from breakfast cereal to candy bars. These dyes are thought to cause a variety of health problems.

As scientific tests reveal more about the effects of food processing on the body, government regulations are increasingly being modified to protect consumers. However, you can become informed yourself by reading labels and asking questions.

CONTROLLING YOUR BODY MASS

The total amount of food you need depends on a number of factors. The most significant one is your level of activity. If you are physically active, you will need more food than if you are inactive. Your food requirements also depend on the amount of energy you use to keep your internal systems, such as circulation and respiration, functioning. This amount of energy, called **basal metabolic rate**, varies from person to person and depends on age, sex, size, and secretions from glands such as the thyroid. You probably know people who eat constantly but whose body mass never seems to increase. They may have a higher than average metabolic rate.

To control your mass, you must balance your eating (your energy intake) with your activity (your energy output). Energy levels in activity, as in food, are measured in kilojoules. For example, 20 french fries contain 1300 kJ of energy. It would take 30 min of jogging at 15 km/h to use up this energy. When you know the energy value of the foods you eat, you can adjust your level of activity accordingly.

The following section will help you understand some of the reasons why you can become too heavy. It will also show you how to determine your ideal mass and suggest practical ways to reduce or increase it.

Why Some People are Too Heavy

There are many complex reasons why people cannot always control their intake of food or output of energy. An abundance of food, the comforts of our society, social pressures, and family eating habits can all contribute to overeating. Emotional, psychological, and physical problems may also cause uncontrolled gain in mass.

In Canada, we live in a comfortable society with an abundance of food and a high standard of living. Studies have shown that about 50% of Canadian adults are too heavy. Well-heated homes and apartments and lightweight and warm clothing have reduced the amount of energy needed to maintain normal body temperature. If the body is kept warm by clothing and room temperature, less energy is used. The many time-saving and labour-saving inventions that are available today demand little physical effort. The less active a person is, the more likely that person is to increase in mass.

Food is an important part of social activities. When you give a party, you want to have good food to offer your guests. When you go to a party, you expect to eat well. Eating at a restaurant with a friend or a group of friends is a common social practice. Often, the food you eat on these occasions is additional to the food you eat at regular meals and it tends to contain a high number of kilojoules. If you take in rich food too frequently, your mass will increase.

People who are inactive are more likely to gain in mass.

Many of your eating habits begin at home. The pattern of eating a family develops is based on a number of factors. Two important considerations are the amount of money it can spend on food and the cost and availability of the food. Family food habits established when you are a child have a strong influence on the sort and amount of food you choose to eat now. If your family enjoys snacking on chips, popcorn, and soft drinks when watching television, you will likely do the same thing. If your parents are concerned about food additives and nutritional value, you will probably be aware of what your food contains.

Cultural background is another important influence on eating habits. Some cultures prefer rich foods as part of their daily diet. Many cultures serve rich traditional foods, particularly during holidays and celebrations. The amount of food a person normally eats can also vary from culture to culture. People from countries such as China are amazed at how much food North Americans consume.

Time is an important factor in determining what people eat. Men and women who work outside of their homes may have limited time for cooking. Some families rely on takeout foods that can be quickly prepared. Others may eat in restaurants two or three times a week. Unfortunately, the food that is most easily obtained is often high in basic food energy but low in essential nutrients.

Many people eat not only when they are physically hungry but when they are unhappy or insecure. Often a habit of overeating develops that is difficult to change. Overeating can lead to excess body mass and further unhappy feelings. Once the pattern is established, it is difficult to break.

Inherited traits can also contribute to excess body mass. Factors that influence the mass of the body are the rate at which food energy is burned and the type of body the person has. In rare cases, a glandular disorder may influence the rate at which food is burned. Body type may also determine a person's athletic ability and his or her participation in physical activities. The less active a person is, the more likely he or she is to put on body fat. If a person has inherited physical characteristics that make increasing body mass easy, maintaining an ideal mass may be difficult.

The effects of the emotions on eating habits.

Approximate Height and Mass Chart

Height (in cm)	Mass (in kg) 13 Years Male	13 Years Female	14 Years Male	14 Years Female	15 Years Male	15 Years Female
132	28.5					
134	30	32				
136	31.5	32.5				
138	33	34				
140	33.5	35.5	33.5	36		
142	35.5	37	35.5	37.5	36	
144	36.5	38	37	39.5	37.5	41
146	38	39.5	38.5	41.5	39	42.5
148	39.5	40.5	40	42.5	40	44.5
150	40.5	42.5	41	44	41	46
152	42	44	42.5	46	43	47.5
154	43	45.5	44	47	44.5	48.5
156	45	47	46	48.5	46.5	50.5
158	47.5	48.5	48	49.5	48	51.5
160	48.5	50	49.5	51	49.5	52.5
162	50	51.5	51	52.5	51.5	53.5
164	52.5	53.5	53	54	53.5	55
166	53	55	54	55	55	56
168	54	57	56	57	57.5	57.5
170	56	58	58	59	59	59.5
172		59	60	60	60	61
174			61	60.5	62	61.5
176			63.5	61	64.5	62
178			65	61.5	65.5	62.5
180			66.5	62	67.5	63
182					69	
184					70	
186					71.5	
188					72.5	

Measuring Body Mass

It is difficult to measure body fat accurately without the use of technical and expensive equipment. However, here are four tests that can be done easily and quickly. No one of these methods should be used by itself. Try all of the tests; if you fail two or more, you are probably not at your ideal mass.

A. Height-Mass Test

Height-mass charts are the most common method of determining your ideal mass. Such a chart should use the factors of age, height, and sex. Even then it is only a rough guide, because it may not consider body build.

On the chart you will find your height and mass for your age and sex. If you are a light-boned person, subtract 3 kg from the mass indicated. If you are a heavy-boned person, add 3 kg.

B. The Mirror Test

Look at yourself in the mirror. Stand back and check your overall appearance. Then look especially at areas such as the abdomen, legs, arms, and buttocks, where fat is often stored. If fat is starting to accumulate in one or more areas, it might be wise to start controlling your mass now.

C. Ruler Test

Lie on your back and place a ruler in the middle of your abdomen, over your navel and pointed toward your head and feet. The ruler should touch both your ribs and your lower abdomen. If the ruler only touches one of these areas, or neither, you may have too much fat in the abdominal area.

D. Pinch Test

Just under 50% of all body fat is located under the skin surface. The measurement of fat in the triceps is a good indication of the amount of your body fat. With the thumb and forefinger of one hand, gently pinch the back of your partner's arm. With a ruler in the other hand, measure the width of the pinched skin. Do this twice and average the results. Measurements over 2.0 cm for males and 2.5 for females indicate a level of body fat that is too high.

How to Interpret your Test Results

Now that you have tried these four tests, how do you determine whether you should start a program to control your body mass? If you failed two or more of the tests, you should develop a plan for yourself that includes an increase in your physical activity and a reduction in the amount of high energy food that you eat.

Even if you find yourself in good condition after trying these tests, it is a good idea to establish good eating and exercise habits early. These habits will make it easier for you to maintain your body in later life. If you could look into a mirror of the future, what would you see?

Reducing Your Body Mass

In order to lose extra body fat, you must take in a lower number of kilojoules of food energy than your body needs for its activities. However, before starting to reduce you should see a doctor to find out if there are any physical reasons why you should not go on a diet or exercise program. A doctor may also help you understand the reason for your problem and provide a good reducing plan. Then, discuss your diet plans with your parents. Ask them and your friends to help you stay away from rich foods.

An effective meal and snack plan is essential to losing extra body mass. You should select foods from all four food groups, but select foods that have fewer kilojoules. For example, choose skim milk instead of whole milk and baked potatoes instead of french fries. Small quantities of nourishing food between meals will help to ease hunger pains. Just be sure you do not increase the total amount of food energy taken in.

Remember that you should increase your energy output. You can make some simple changes in your daily habits to extend your level of physical activity. For example, stand rather than sit, walk up stairs rather than use escalators or elevators. Do not oversleep. When you sleep you burn up very little energy. Taking up a sports activity will also increase the amount of energy you use.

Some people may not notice any change for as long as two or three weeks, regardless of how strict their diet is. The reason for this is that as fat is lost from the cells it is replaced by water which may remain in the cells for some time. Eventually it is lost rapidly. It is discouraging if early in your diet there is no loss in mass. However, if you can last for just two or three months, there should be a substantial reduction. You should also be aware that a period of loss is often followed by a period when there is no loss, but that you will eventually begin to lose again. Keep a chart of your progress and reward yourself for keeping to your plan. It is recommended that you lose no more than 1 kg per week when dieting. Losing more than this can be dangerous to your health.

Food Choices

Cut Out	Cut Down	Substitute
milk shakes		two per cent milk
whole milk	number of glasses	or skim milk
french fries		plain baked potato
regular soft drinks	calorie-reduced	soda water, fruit juice
double-sized hamburger		regular (single patty) hamburger
chili dog		plain hot dog
potato salad	size of portion	tossed salad — no dressing
Danish pastry		whole wheat bread
	peanut butter	hard cheese
	milk pudding	make them with skim milk
	rich ice cream	ice milk
fruit-flavoured yogurt		plain yogurt with fresh fruit
buttered popcorn		plain popcorn
candy bar		25 peanuts
	mayonnaise	lettuce (in sandwiches)
sugar and cream in coffee or tea	coffee or tea	plain tea with lemon or bouillon
	french toast with syrup	french toast with applesauce
cream-filled cookie		raisin/oatmeal cookies (2)
	cream soups	clear soups
fried chicken		baked or broiled chicken
	jam, honey	cheese slice

YOUR BODY BUILD

Your body build (bone structure and shape) is inherited from your parents along with all of your other physical characteristics. The three extremes of body type are:

1. *ectomorph*—has light bones and very little fat. Ectomorphs are thin all of their lives.
2. *endomorph*—has a heavy bone structure and pads of soft rounded flesh. Even if an endomorph diets, he or she will never look as thin as an ectomorph.
3. *mesomorph*—has medium-heavy bones and little fat. These people also have well-developed muscles. Many athletes are mesomorphic in build.

Most people are combinations of these three types, although you should be able to tell what your basic shape is. In planning a diet to lose weight, you should keep your basic body type in mind and set a goal that is realistic.

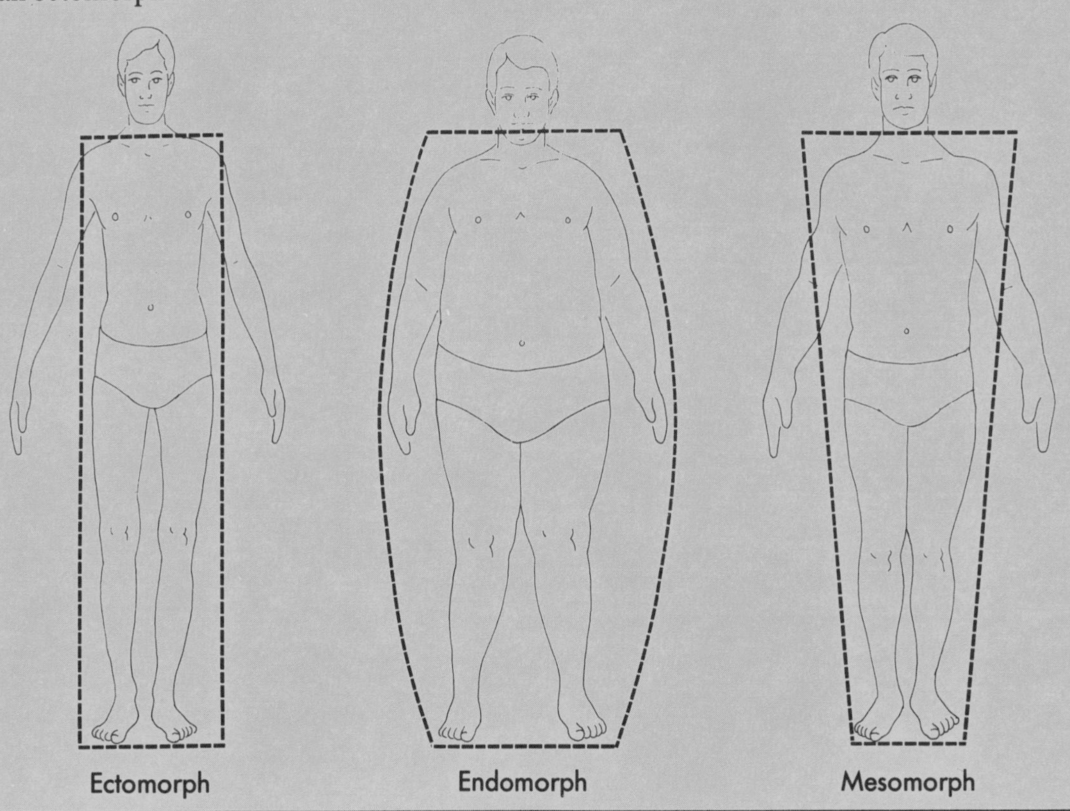

REDUCING METHODS

Special Diets and Diet Aids

Every few years a new diet is promoted as the solution to excess body mass. Thousands of people have tried grapefruit, high protein, banana, high fat, and low carbohydrate diets. These diets are often appealing because you do not have to think much to follow them. However, they are short-term solutions. They also do not provide balanced nutrition so that even if you lose some body fat, you may damage your health.

The multi-million dollar business of diet aids exists because people want an effortless method of dieting. Most of these methods are ineffective and remain on the market only a short time. The following are some of the techniques used in this business:

1. **Diuretics** are drugs that are used to reduce the amount of water, not fat, in the body. This water loss is replaced soon after because the body needs to maintain a fluid balance. Steam baths, bath salts, and sauna baths are also devices used to lose water, but the effect is only temporary. These methods should only be used under strict medical supervision.
2. **Amphetamines** are drugs used to decrease your appetite. They can be dangerous to your health and should be taken only under medical guidance.

Discuss why the reducing methods shown here are not good choices.

3. Pills containing sugar can be taken half an hour before a meal to raise the blood sugar and so decrease your appetite. These pills are very expensive, especially when you consider the same effect can be obtained by drinking a glass of fruit juice or by eating fresh fruit.

4. Some diet gadgets and machines that claim to "trim away fat" make use of the fact that fat cells in the body are high in water content. If some of this water is removed by sweating or pressure, 1 or 2 cm may be temporarily lost from a certain area of the body. However, this fat returns when liquids are taken in or when the pressure has been lessened.

Special diets and diet aids are tempting to try because they promise a quick, painless solution to your problems. Do not be taken in by the advertising. Although you may become thinner temporarily, you are not curing the cause of excess body mass. It is likely that you will gain back what you have lost and you may injure your health in the process.

SUGGESTIONS FOR DECREASING BODY MASS

Everyone needs ideas and motivation to diet. Here are some ideas that may help you succeed:

1. Drink a glass of water 5 to 10 min before beginning a meal.
2. Start your dinner with a salad but use a dressing low in food energy.
3. Do not use excessive amounts of salt.
4. Use a smaller plate.
5. Cut down on fats, especially animal fats. Cut down on meats.
6. Drink diet sodas, if you must drink pop.
7. Diet with a friend.
8. Minimize your intake of all fried foods.
9. Reduce amount of desserts.
10. Do not eat while watching television.
11. If you crave a sweet, eat a carrot.
12. Chew sugar-free gum (25 kJ per stick).
13. Eat slowly and taste your food thoroughly.

Keep a chart of your progress.

Too Little Body Mass

You may feel unattractive because you lack flesh and muscle. It may be that all the food energy you take in is being used in growing tall, or you may have a high metabolic rate. Perhaps you simply do not eat enough. Whatever the reason, a proper diet and exercise program can help you look the way you want to.

The best method to increase your mass and improve your appearance is to eat a balanced diet that includes more foods high in energy. You should also start an exercise program based on weight resistance (see page 21). Such a program will not only increase your muscle and, consequently, your mass, it will give you an attractive appearance. Both boys and girls can follow this course of action with success.

A Very Serious Illness

Sometimes people become obsessed with the idea of being thin. Usually they begin by thinking that they will be more attractive if they lose a few kilograms. After they have lost that amount, they decide to keep on dieting because the loss does not seem quite enough. They continue to feel that losing just a little more will make them truly attractive. When people become so concerned about being thin that it is the main focus of their lives, they have an illness called **anorexia nervosa**.

This illness is a very serious one, as drastic reduction in mass can severely damage the body. Because anorexics try to live on a minimum amount of food, they become very undernourished. It is crucial to recognize symptoms of this illness at an early stage and seek medical help.

Energy Value of Some Foods

Food	Energy (in kJ)
Whole Milk (250 mL)	660
Skim milk (250 mL)	380
Chocolate malted milk shake (250 mL)	1060
Hamburger on a bun	1770
Chocolate cake, iced (1 piece)	980
French fries (10 pieces)	650
Pizza (1 piece)	1675
Fried chicken (1 piece)	370-650
Boiled egg	330
Celery (1 stalk)	20
Carrot (1 medium)	80

GOOD NUTRITION— A LIFETIME HABIT

The food habits you develop as a young person are important in two ways. First of all, as you are at a time in your life when your body is changing very rapidly, good nutrition will ensure that you will develop to your fullest potential and that you will look and feel your best while you are growing. Second, the habits you establish now are likely to continue as you get older. By learning to choose nutritious foods during adolescence, you will contribute to your future health and appearance.

The food habits you develop as a young person are important.

FOR REVIEW

Key Ideas

- Good nutrition is especially important during adolescence because many changes are taking place in your body.
- The important elements in a nutritious diet are carbohydrates, fats, proteins, minerals, vitamins, water and fibre.
- In order to be properly nourished, it is important to be aware of what you are eating.
- The total amount of food you need to maintain an ideal body mass depends on your level of activity, your basal metabolic rate and how much food you eat.
- There are many complex reasons why people cannot always control their intake of food or output of energy.
- In order to reduce your body mass you must consume less energy than your body needs for its activities; in order to gain mass you must take in more energy than your body needs for its activities.

Questions and Activities

1. Why are some sources of food better for supplying energy than others?
2. Why must people who follow a vegetarian diet be particularly careful of the food choices they make?
3. Briefly give eight reasons why people can become too heavy.
4. List the two basic ways to lose body mass and explain why they are effective.
5. List the foods that are served in the school cafeteria and poll the class to find out what foods are most popular and why. Consider the price, appearance, and nutritional value. What have you learned about the eating habits of your classmates?
6. Make a collection of food labels from cans, jars and packages. Compare the contents of fresh, frozen and canned foods. Make a list of nutritional foods for a shopping list.
7. Write a report on the use of additives in foods. Consider both the pros and cons of additives.
8. Do a week's food shopping (on paper) for a family of 4 or 5 with a minimal amount of money. Try to provide for a balanced diet.
9. As a class project, outline a campaign to convince teen-agers to improve their eating habits. Your campaign might include advertising on radio and television and wall posters.
10. Plan a meatless meal. Make sure there are foods high in protein to meet the daily requirement adequately. What is the difference in cost between this meal and a meal with meat?
11. You are invited to a friend's place for dinner and you are served a great quantity of food. You know that it exceeds the kilojoule count you are maintaining on your diet. How should you handle the situation?
12. List ten ways you can help a friend to diet.

UNIT TWO

HOW YOU GROW AND WHY

CHAPTER FIVE

THE BEGINNING OF LIFE

THE REPRODUCTIVE SYSTEMS

The development of new life from two tiny cells is an awesome and intricate process. It is often called the "miracle of life." The reproductive organs that enable you to create new life are formed several months before your own birth. However, they remain largely inactive until **puberty** when **hormones** released by your **pituitary gland** cause the sexual organs to mature, and you become capable of reproduction.

Females have two **ovaries**, the organs which produce egg cells called **ova**. When a girl has reached puberty, an egg or ovum is generally released once every 28 days. This release of a ripe egg, called **ovulation**, is controlled by hormones. At the time of ovulation, a girl may experience a slight rise in temperature, pain in the abdomen, a change in vaginal discharge, and perhaps slight spotting. Not everyone will experience these symptoms; as a result, ovulation is often difficult to predict.

As the ovum is developing in one of the ovaries, the lining of the uterus **(endometrium)** thickens. Once released, the ovum is propelled by small hairs called **cilia** along the **Fallopian tube** toward the **uterus**. If it is not fertilized, that is, not penetrated by a **sperm** cell, it dies and is expelled along with the lining of the uterus through the **cervix** and the **vagina** to the outside of the body. This flow of blood and tissue is called **menstruation**.

The Reproductive System of the Female

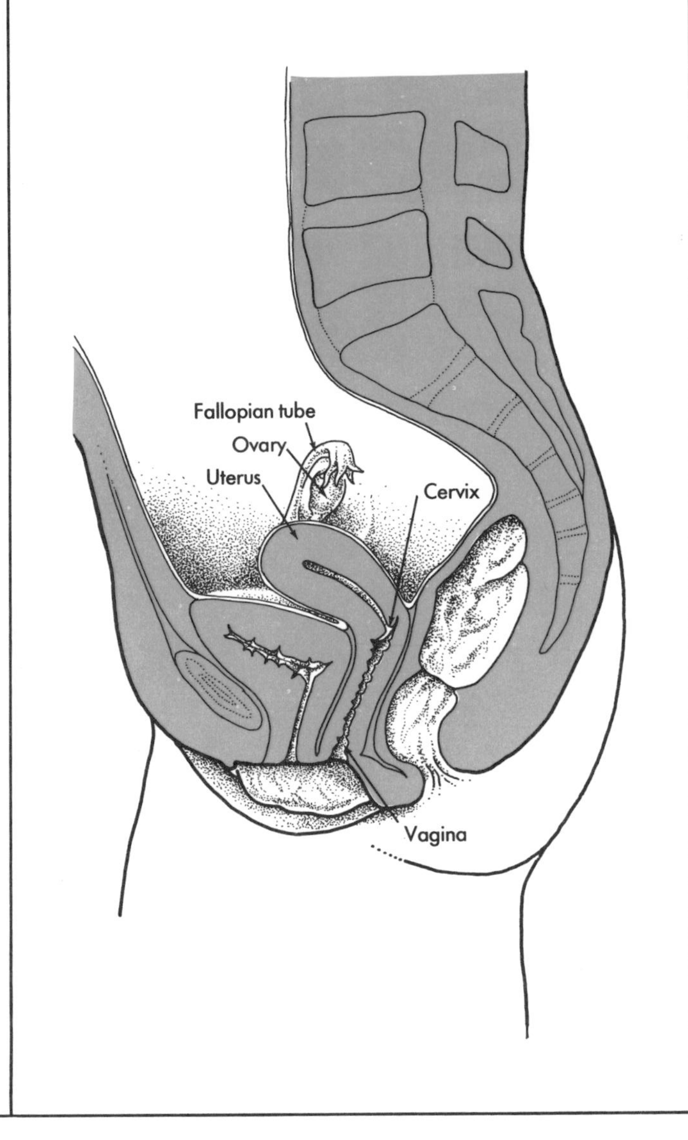

The most important reproductive organs in males are two glands called **testes**. When a boy reaches puberty, they begin to produce the sperm cells needed to fertilize the ova of the female. These glands are protected in a sack of skin called the **scrotum**. As the sperm are produced, they are temporarily stored in the **epididymis**, small tubules that lie on top and alongside the testes. When **ejaculation** occurs, sperm are projected along the **vas deferens** (sperm ducts) and past the **seminal vesicles** which add a fluid nutrient. Sperm and fluid then move through the **prostate gland**, where a milky alkaline substance is added to neutralize acids. This mixture of fluids and sperm, called **semen**, then travels down the **urethra** and out the opening of the penis.

During sexual intercourse, ejaculated sperm move from the vagina of the female through the cervix into the uterus. From the uterus, the sperm, shaped somewhat like tadpoles, propel themselves with great speed up the Fallopian tube to meet the ovum. They can reach the ovum in 1 to 2 h. Since sperm can stay alive for up to three days, they do not need to arrive exactly at the time of ovulation. The ovum, however, must be fertilized within two days or it will disintegrate.

An ejaculate of seminal fluid contains about 300 million sperm. This seems wasteful, but most sperm do not make it to the egg. Many sperm are needed around the egg so that the enzyme they give off will break down the cells and wall of the egg, allowing one sperm to penetrate.

The Reproductive System of the Male

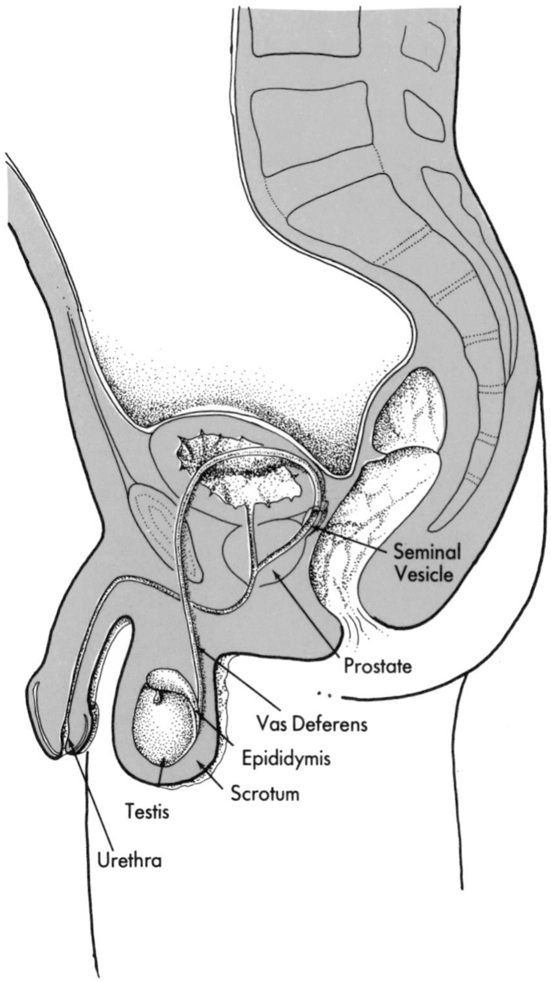

CONCEPTION AND THE DEVELOPING BABY

Conception is the joining together of egg and sperm. As the fertilized egg or **zygote** moves toward the uterus, it begins to divide into numerous cells. By the time it reaches the uterus it is a ball of many cells, called a **morula**. The morula develops an inner cavity with a group of cells on one side. Now called a **blastocyst**, this ball of cells implants or attaches itself to the wall of the uterus. Over the next nine months, this cellular structure will develop into a human baby.

Once the blastocyst burrows into the lining of the uterus, it is called an **embryo**. A system then develops to nourish this growing embryo. Blood vessels form a **placenta**, an organ that makes possible the transfer of food and oxygen from the mother's blood stream to the baby's blood stream and the return of waste products from the baby to the mother. The placenta is connected to the embryo by the **umbilical cord** through which the nutrients and wastes flow. At the same time, a sac containing **amniotic fluid** forms around the embryo to protect and cushion it.

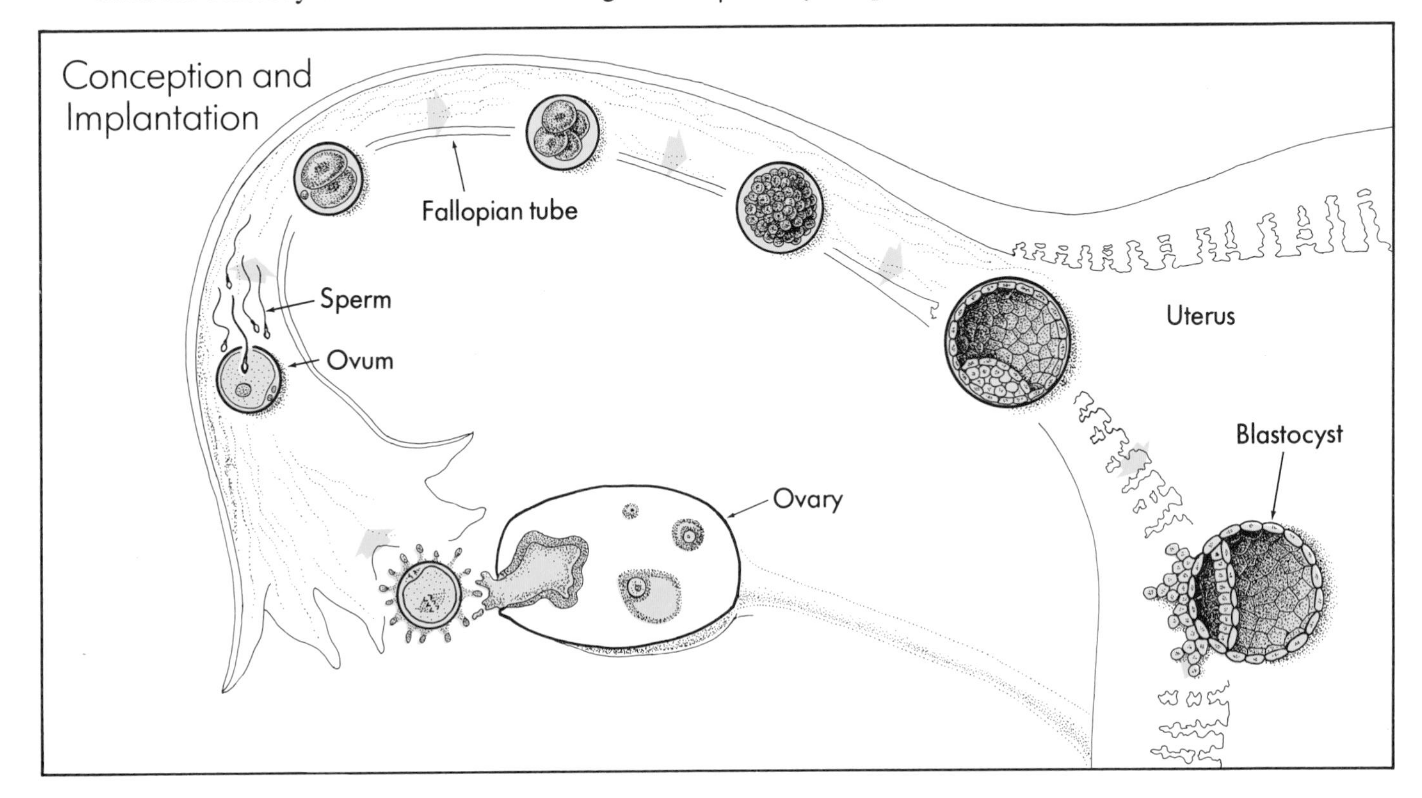

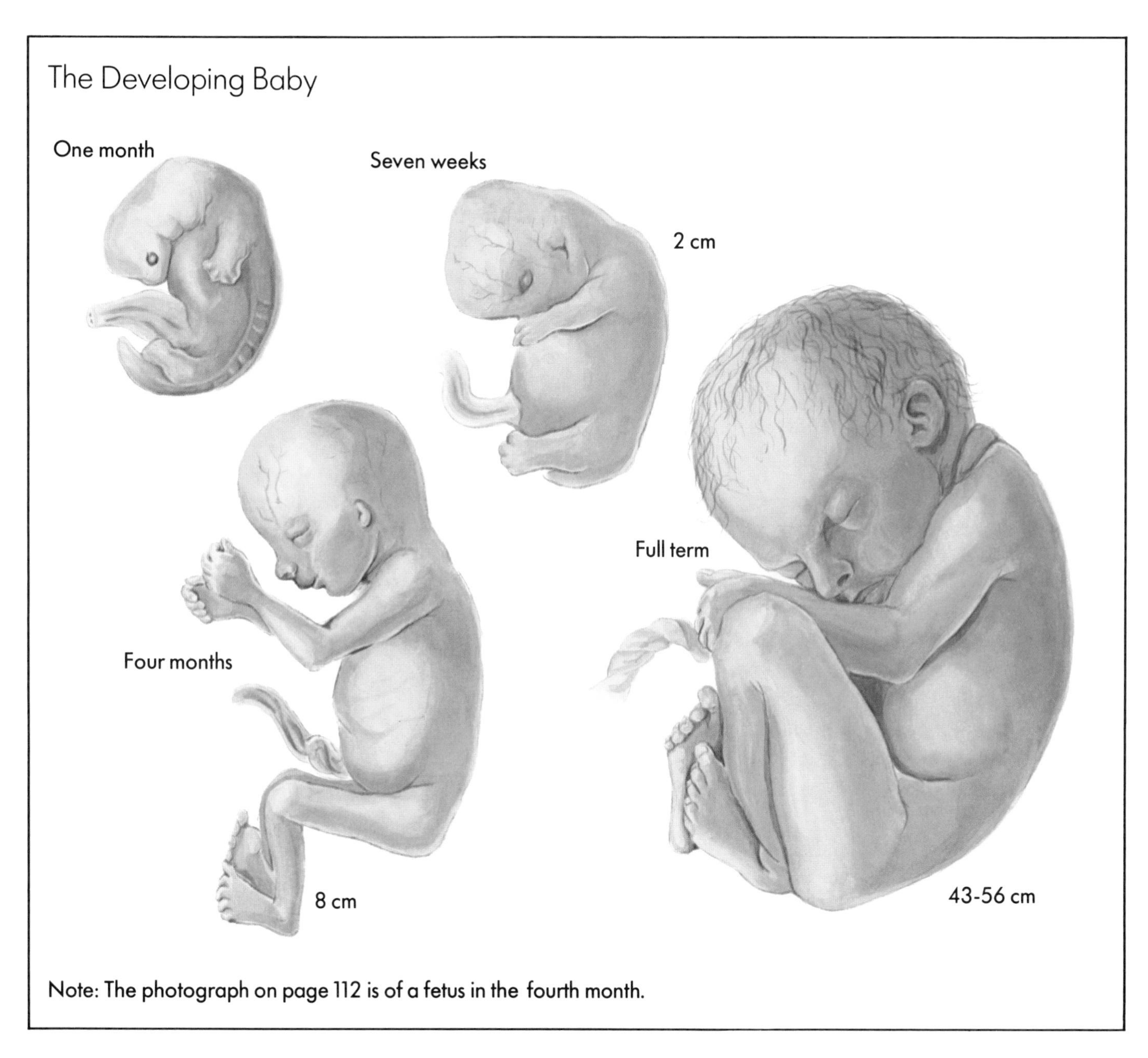

Note: The photograph on page 112 is of a fetus in the fourth month.

By the end of the second month, the embryo, now called a **fetus**, is 3 to 4 cm long, with the head making up half the total length. Ears, eyes, nose, mouth, arms, and legs have developed. Genital organs have appeared but the sex cannot yet be determined with accuracy. The heart begins to beat on about the twenty-second day but it is still so small that it cannot be heard easily until the fourth or fifth month.

By the end of the fourth month, the mother can feel the fetus' movements. This is called quickening. Fingernails and toenails have developed and the sex is discernible. The fetus is half its expected birth length but its mass is only about 70 g.

In the fifth month, the uterus expands to reach the height of the mother's navel. The fetus is now about 30 cm long and has a mass of approximately 500 g. In the amniotic sac it moves about freely. It may be sucking its thumb and may even have hiccups. Almost all of the baby teeth have begun to form by this time. However, it is not until the end of the sixth month that the fetus has a small chance of survival outside the womb, since the respiratory system is now sufficiently developed.

During the last three months, the developing baby gains a great deal of mass through the increase in fat and muscle tissue. These tissues protect the inner organs after birth and cushion the body during the birth process.

CONCEPTION CONTROL

Conception control may be used for a variety of reasons. Some couples may decide not to have children. Others may wish to limit the number of children or space their arrival. Occasionally, some women should not have children because their health is poor.

References to the use of devices to control conception go back to Egyptian civilization 4000 years ago. Today, a variety of methods is used to plan pregnancy. Conception control can be achieved in the following ways:

a. Abstaining from sexual activity.
b. Interrupting the passage of sperm.
c. Interrupting the passage of the ovum.
d. Preventing the egg from being released.
e. Preventing the fertilized egg from being implanted in the uterus.
f. Having sexual intercourse when the ovum is not ripe.
g. Killing the sperm by spermicides.

In the chart, you will find information on various types of conception control. Try to match each method in the chart with one of the seven categories listed above.

Methods of Conception Control

Method	Effectiveness	Advantages	Disadvantages
Natural			
Abstinence	excellent	no cost	None
Rhythm	poor to fair	no cost	A woman must have a regular cycle to use effectively
Withdrawal	poor	no cost	Difficult to withdraw; some sperm may be released prior to ejaculation
Chemical			
Foam	good	Available without prescription	Continual expense
Pills	excellent	Highly effective; regulates menstrual cycle	Cost; possible side effects; must be taken daily
Mechanical			
Intrauterine Device	excellent	Minimal cost; requires no motivation	Side effects; may be expelled
Condom	very good	Available without prescription	Must apply just before intercourse; continual expense
Diaphragm (with cream or jelly)	very good	No side effects inexpensive	Must insert before intercourse
Surgical			
Tubal Ligation	excellent	Is highly effective	May be permanent
Vasectomy	excellent	Is highly effective	May be permanent

PREGNANCY

Signs and Symptoms of Pregnancy

How does a woman know if she is pregnant? A number of possible signs of pregnancy include a missed period, tiredness, nausea, frequent urination, and tender, swollen breasts. In order to be certain of pregnancy in its early stages, the woman must be tested. The standard test given by doctors does not indicate pregnancy until about 14 days after the menstrual period is expected. There are also drugstore tests which may determine pregnancy within 9 days after conception. They provide faster but perhaps less accurate results.

Health Care During Pregnancy

The health of the developing baby is directly related to the health of the mother. As a result, health care during this time is essential. Regular visits to the doctor will ensure that problems are quickly detected and treated. During these visits, mass and blood pressure are recorded, since a significant rise in either would be dangerous to the mother.

Pregnant women should eat about the same amount of food as usual, but they should ensure that their diet includes all of the food nutrients. Women who have a poor diet during pregnancy tend to have more miscarriages, stillbirths, and smaller babies than those with nutritious diets. Moderate exercise during pregnancy is also beneficial. It develops a good appetite and improves blood circulation, muscle tone, and digestion. Women who keep active during pregnancy are more likely to have a positive mental outlook.

Although the blood of the mother does not mix directly with the blood of the baby, substances in the blood pass from the mother to the developing fetus. For example, the mother provides the child with nutrients and oxygen. Unfortunately, harmful materials can also be transmitted to the baby. Nicotine, tars from smoking, alcohol, and drugs can cross to the fetus. Certain diseases carried in the mother's blood (German measles, syphilis, and influenza) can cause severe injury. Since her health directly affects the health of her baby, a mother should be especially careful to avoid disease and unnecessary drugs during pregnancy. The early months of pregnancy, when the major systems and structures of the baby are developing, are the most critical time.

The mother's body nurtures the growing child, but the father should recognize that he has an important role to play during the pregnancy. Since the health of the baby depends on the health of the mother, the father should provide continuing emotional and physical support. By understanding what is happening to her, he will know better what she needs. Sometimes a man is so much in sympathy with his wife's condition, he will experience symptoms similar to hers. He can

TWINS

Two thirds of all twins are fraternal; that is, they originate from two separate ova. They will be as different, therefore, as any two siblings. One third of twins are identical. Because identical twins are the product of a single fertilized ovum which divides into two, they are always the same sex. The role heredity plays in twinning is not completely understood. A family history of twins increases somewhat the chances of having fraternal twins. Identical twins cannot be predicted.

One in sixty thousand births results in Siamese twins. Siamese twins originate from one egg and one sperm that does not completely split to produce identical twins. The twins are, therefore, joined together at one or more points on the body. Often, if the twins do not share vital organs, they can be sucessfully separated.

Occasionally, multiple births of more than two occur. Perhaps the most famous of these births is that of the Dionne quintuplets. What was unusual about the Dionnes was that they were all identical, that is, they came from one egg and one sperm that divided five times, producing five identical girls.

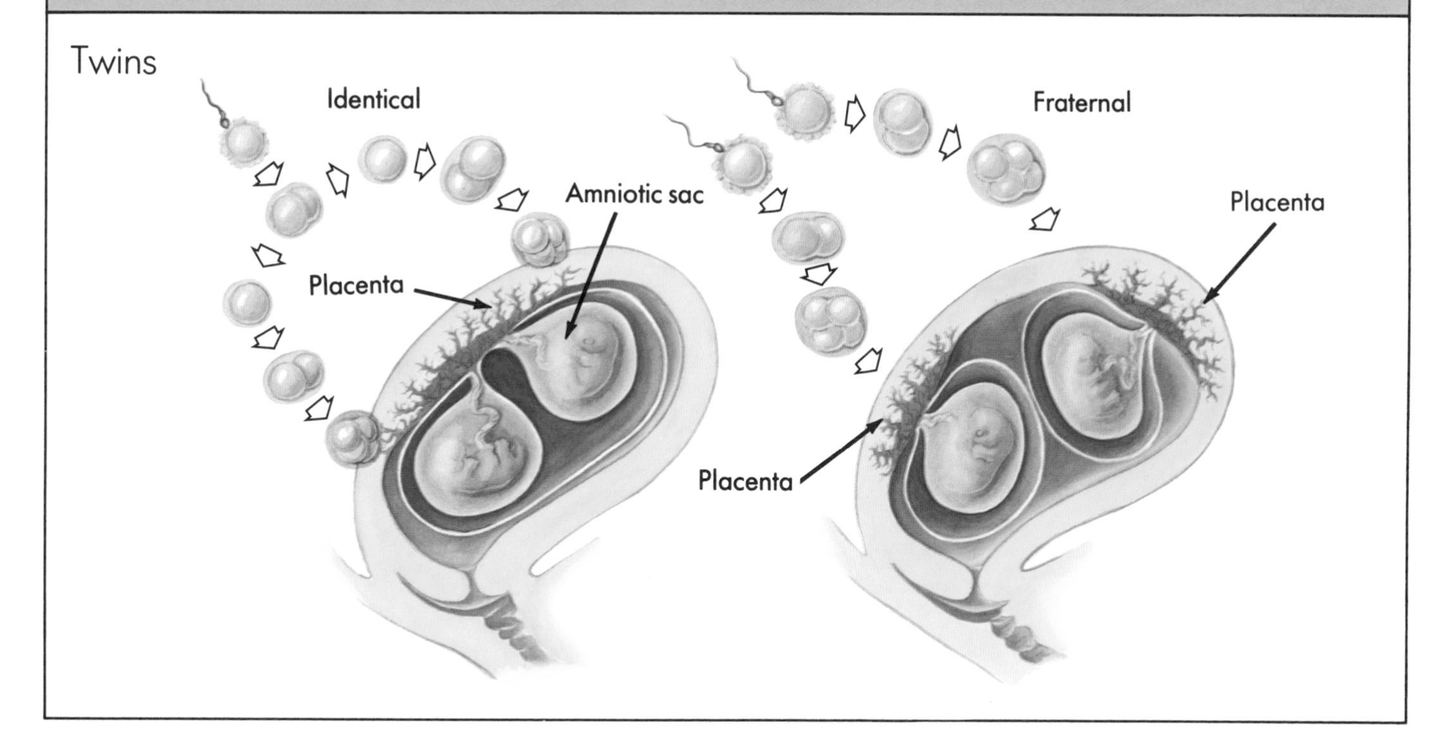

attend pre-natal classes which will inform him of all the changes taking place and their effects. Such classes will also prepare him if he wishes to attend the birth.

People's feelings about pregnancy are often complex and changeable. Both the mother and the father have to adjust to the idea of being parents. Sometimes they will enjoy discussing and observing the changes in the mother and at other times they may worry about the normal development of their child. They may look forward to the birth as the start of a new adventure, or they may worry about their ability to be good parents. Pregnancy will bring a permanent change to their lives and to their relationship.

AMNIOCENTESIS

A technique called **amniocentesis** has been developed for testing the health of the fetus very early in the pregnancy. A sampling of amniotic fluid is taken from the mother through a needle inserted in the uterus. This test can determine the sex of the child and possible heredity problems. It is not regarded as a routine test, but it is used when there is the possibility of certain hereditary diseases or when the pregnant woman is over the age of 35 and the risk of Down's Syndrome increases.

HOW THE SEX OF A CHILD IS DETERMINED

Each human cell normally contains 46 chromosomes. However, through a process called **meiosis**, the sperm cells and egg cells which develop for reproductive purposes contain only twenty-three chromosomes each. One of these chromosomes determines the sex of the child. The chromosome contained by the sperm can be either an X chromosome (female) or a Y (male). Each ovum contains only an X chromosome. If an X-containing sperm unites with the ovum, a female child (XX) will result. If a Y-containing sperm unites with the egg, a male child (XY) will develop. As you can see, the father's sperm determines the sex of the offspring.

The chromosomes have thousands of separate parts called **genes**. Genes determine your physical characteristics—eye colour, hair texture, and height. Since half your chromosomes have come from your mother and half from your father, your physical inheritance comes equally from both. However, some genes are said to be dominant and others, recessive. Genes that are dominant will generally determine a person's characteristics. If both parents have brown eyes, their children will most likely have brown eyes since this characteristic is dominant. However, if both parents also carry a gene for blue eyes, one or more of their children may have blue eyes.

Exercise during pregnancy is important because it improves the health of the mother-to-be.

THE RH FACTOR

About 85% of the population have a particular characteristic in their blood called the **Rh factor**. The other 15% do not. Those with the Rh factor are said to have Rh positive blood; those without, are said to have Rh negative blood.

If the blood of a pregnant woman is Rh negative, and the blood of the fetus she is carrying is Rh positive, there is a danger that future babies will become seriously ill and possibly die. At the time of birth (or miscarriage), some blood from the baby mixes with blood from the mother. The baby's Rh positive blood triggers the mother's Rh negative blood to produce antibodies, the same substances that protect the body from disease. During subsequent pregnancies, antibodies in the mother's blood circulate to the fetus and attack its blood.

Women with Rh negative blood can protect their future children if they are injected immediately after birth or miscarriage with a substance which destroys these antibodies. The mother's blood then becomes safe for new life.

CHILDBIRTH

The effort of giving birth to a baby is known as labour. The average duration of labour in the first birth is 12 h and in subsequent births, 6 to 8 h. There are certain warnings that labour has started or about to begin. Amniotic fluid leaks from the uterus. There may be slight bleeding and a feeling of tightness around the abdomen. The actual onset of childbirth is indicated by rhythmical contractions of the uterus occurring at increasingly shortened intervals.

During the first stage of labour, the cervix dilates. The contractions of the uterus exert pressure on the baby and amniotic sac, forcing

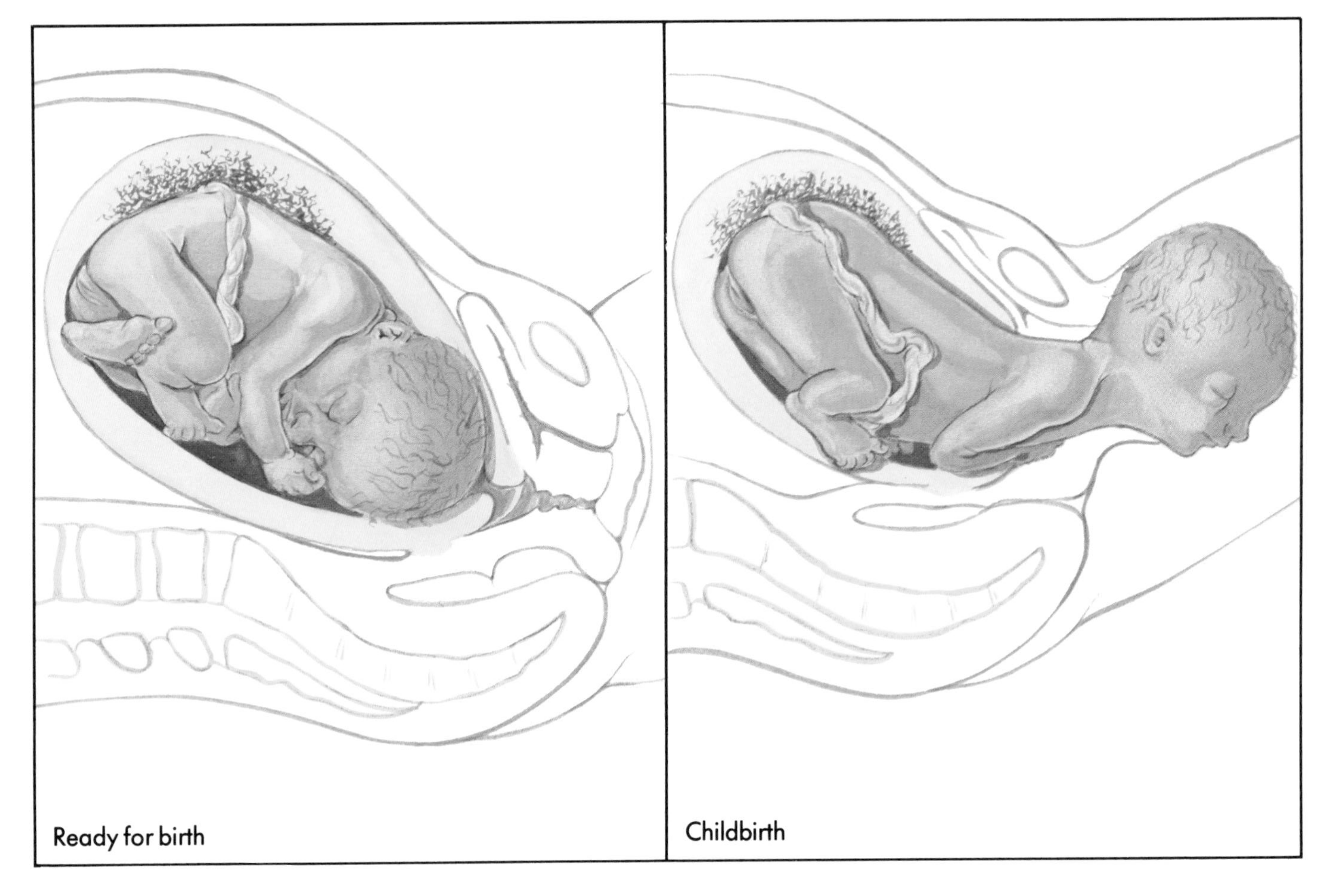

Ready for birth

Childbirth

them gradually downwards and into the cervix. The cervix slowly opens and the amniotic sac breaks.

During the second stage, the cervix is fully opened and the baby is pushed head first through the birth canal. The final stage includes the expulsion of afterbirth (the placenta, umbilical cord, and fluids).

After birth, **mucus** is removed from the baby's nose and mouth and the umbilical cord is cut and clamped. The baby can now eat, excrete, and breathe on its own. Silver nitrate drops are put in the eyes for protection against the effects of possible sexually transmitted disease. The baby's mass is determined and it is given a physical examination.

About 97% of all babies are born head first. However, the baby sometimes does not drop head first into the cervix, and the legs and buttocks are the first parts delivered. This is called a breech birth. If the baby is too large for the pelvic opening or the placenta is blocking the passage through the birth canal, the doctor will cut the abdominal wall and the uterus to remove it. This operation is called a **Caesarean section**.

The experience of giving birth is unique to each woman and an individual will experience differences in the labour and birth of each of her children. Some women request an anaesthetic to relieve the discomfort of labour. The usual method involves dripping small amounts of a drug into the **epidural canal** near the base of the spine. This is called a regional **anaesthetic**. The pelvis and legs are numbed and the labour proceeds without pain. In the case of a Caesarean delivery, a general anaesthetic is usually given and the woman is unconscious during the birth.

Many women prepare for the birth by attending classes where they are given information on all aspects of pregnancy. They are taught a variety of exercises that will relax them during the birth process. One method, called the La Maze method, involves having the father present as a "coach" for the mother. He helps to relax and encourage her before and during the birth.

A birth technique practised in some hospitals, often called the Leboyer Method, is meant to ease the trauma of the birth experience for the baby. During the delivery, the lights are dim and soft music is played. When born, the baby is placed on the mother's abdomen for about 30 min before the umbilical cord is cut. Once the cord is cut, the baby is put in a bath of water the same temperature as the amniotic fluid. This environment is created to imitate the child's previous home in the uterus.

Women generally decide what method of birth they prefer and discuss it with their doctor ahead of time. More men are actively participating in the birth of their children today, not only during labour, but during the actual delivery.

THE CARE OF YOUNG BABIES

A very special bond develops between the mother and the baby. This **bonding** is believed to begin early in prenatal development when the mother's emotional state may affect the life of the fetus. Immediately after birth, touching, holding, and talking softly to the baby seems to improve its sense of well-being. Many doctors believe that breast-feeding increases the bonding effect between mother and child. However, both father and mother should be involved in the bonding process, since the bonds develop between the child and those who nurture it.

The needs of tiny babies differ greatly from those of adults. Because their organs are so small, they need to eat and to excrete far more often than adults or even older children. The only foods that are safe for young babies to eat are breast milk or specially devised artificial formulas. If a baby is not breast-fed, great care must be taken to sterilize the bottles it uses in order to prevent serious stomach and intestinal disease. Most infants under three months of age need to eat every 3 to 4 h and they need to be changed every 2 to 3 h.

A very small baby sleeps most of the time and needs to. It is during sleep that growth occurs. The first year of life is one of enormous growth. Infants usually triple their birth weight and grow 12 to 15 cm.

Small babies cry when they are uncomfortable. They may be hungry, need changing, or suffer from gas pains. Babies will also cry if they are cold, lonely, or frightened. If you are caring for a baby who is crying, you should try to determine the source of its unhappiness. Remember that cuddling and comforting are just as important to a baby's well-being as attention to its physical needs.

Many books have been written on the subject of baby and child care. Most of these offer good advice and comfort to people who may be nervous about looking after a small baby for the first time. These books are available in inexpensive paperback form and are generally found in any bookstore.

Affection is important to a baby's happiness.

THE CYCLE OF LIFE

As you have read in the preceding pages, the care a young baby receives is very important for its physical and emotional development. People who are well cared for as babies and children have a better chance of becoming happy, healthy adults. In turn, they nurture their own children and the cycle repeats itself.

Playing with young children develops their skills.

FOR REVIEW

Key Ideas

- At puberty your sexual organs mature and you become capable of reproduction.
- After conception, a baby generally develops over a nine month period in the uterus.
- Conception can be controlled in a variety of ways.
- Pregnancy will bring changes to the lives of the mother and father.
- Labour, which is the effort of giving birth to a child, occurs in three stages.
- A variety of methods can be used to facilitate the birth of a child.
- Young babies require special care.

Questions and Activities

1. Why is the health of the mother so important to the development of the fetus?
2. What special care do young infants require?
3. Research and report on the following factors which influence the health of the developing fetus or embryo. Make up slogans that would suggest some of the dangers.
   a. smoking
   b. nutrition
   c. alcohol
   d. drugs
4. There are indications that in the near future we will be able to determine the sex of our children. Surveys show that about 75% of parents want the first and third child to be male. Discuss the possible effects if this were to take place.
5. The following is a list of responsibilities that must be assumed during and after pregnancy. List the ones you think the mother should assume, the ones the father should assume, and the ones both should assume:
   - eating nutritious foods
   - avoiding tobacco, alcohol, or other drugs
   - providing a warm house, good food and clothing
   - feeding the baby
   - changing the baby
   - cuddling the baby
   - planning the baby's room
   - buying equipment for the baby
   - getting up at night
   - attending pre-natal classes.

NO
PARKING
2A.M.-5A.M.
EXCEPT
BY PERMIT
7G

CHAPTER SIX

YOUR ADOLESCENT YEARS

A TIME OF RAPID CHANGE

Adolescence is a unique period in your life when, in a relatively short time, you undergo major physical and emotional changes. You are moving from childhood to adulthood, and you will find yourself developing new interests, attitudes, and concerns. Sometimes you may feel as if you are a brand-new person. The most noticeable signs of change occur in your body. You begin to grow more rapidly than you have in the past and your body starts to mature into that of an adult. It may take time to accept these physical changes and to adjust mentally to a new image in the mirror.

As you move toward adulthood, your relationships with your friends and the adults in your life also begin to change. You may discover that you no longer have anything in common with friends you have had for years. All of a sudden, you may become very interested in the opposite sex. Increasingly, you will want to make your own decisions and take responsibility for them. At times you may disagree with the adults in your life about what you should do; at other times you feel you especially need the support and protection of your home. In either case, you will want to make your feelings known and you will want to have them respected.

In this chapter, you will look at the physical, emotional, and social changes during this period of your life. You will also think about what it means to be male or female and about the kinds of choices and decisions that face you as you become an adult.

Becoming an adult can be an exciting experience.

People grow in different ways.

Endocrine Glands That Promote Growth

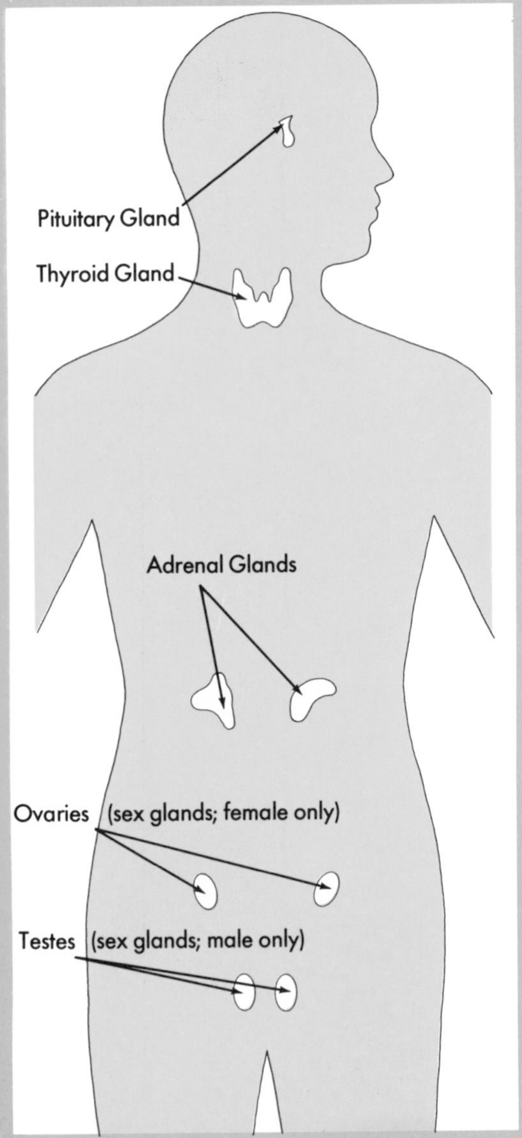

Pituitary Gland
Thyroid Gland
Adrenal Glands
Ovaries (sex glands; female only)
Testes (sex glands; male only)

Endocrine Gland	Hormone	Function
Pituitary	Follicle-stimulating hormone (FSH)	Promotes the production of hormones by the testes and ovaries.
	Growth Hormone	Stimulates the growth of the bones and other tissues.
	Thyrotropin	Stimulates the production of thyroxin and the growth of the thyroid gland.
Ovaries	Estrogen Progesterone	Promotes the development of female sex characteristics.
Testes	Testosterone	Promotes the development of male sex characteristics.
Adrenals	Androgens	Promote rapid growth during adolescence and the development of male genitals.
Thyroid	Thyroxin	Regulates the rate at which cells use up food.

YOUR CHANGING BODY

The physical changes that occur during adolescence result from an increase in the activities of organs called **endocrine glands** which are located throughout the body. Through the release of substances called hormones into the bloodstream, these glands control and stimulate a wide variety of body processes, including growth and maturation.

One of the most important of these glands is the pituitary gland, located on the underside of the brain. The pituitary produces a hormone that causes the bones to grow rapidly during adolescence and a **follicle-stimulating hormone** that stimulates the production of sperm cells in males and ova in females. The pituitary also manufactures a hormone that triggers the testes in boys to produce **testosterone**, the male sex hormone, and the ovaries in girls to produce **estrogen** and **progesterone**, the female sex hormones. These sex hormones are responsible for many of the obvious sexual changes that occur in adolescent boys and girls.

The pituitary is also responsible for a hormone that stimulates the thyroid gland to produce the hormone **thyroxin**. Thyroxin influences the rate at which foods are used in the cells. If too much thyroxin is produced, food is used up too quickly and much energy is produced. This results in a loss of mass. If too little thyroxin is produced, food is used too slowly and there is a lack of energy and a gain in mass.

The **adrenal glands**, located on top of the kidneys, produce androgen sex hormones or **androgens**. Androgens, like the growth hormone produced by the pituitary gland, stimulate rapid growth during adolescence. Because boys produce more androgens than girls, their growth is greater. In males, these adrenal hormones also work with testosterone to promote the development of the genitals.

Everyone has a unique physical timetable. This means that these changes occur at different times for different people. You will have noticed a wide range in the height, mass, and development of your classmates. Your rate of growth is influenced by inherited physical traits, the nature of the environment, and your sex. Girls, for example, will mature sooner than boys. It is natural to worry about your rate of growth, particularly if you are developing faster or slower than most of your friends. However, most people have reached their adult height by about the age of eighteen. Your parents will probably tell you they grew in the same way.

Physical Changes in Boys

During adolescence, boys grow on the average about 20 cm and gain 20 kg. The shoulders widen, the chest broadens, and the muscles develop. Pains in joints often occur during periods of rapid growth, because the bones lengthen more quickly than the muscles and ligaments. Until you adjust to this new growth, you may feel awkward and unco-ordinated. You may also notice that your voice goes from high to low as you talk. Because the size of your voice box (larynx) is increasing, your vocal cords are lengthening. Very shortly you will have a voice that is deeper in sound.

As the body grows, so do the genitals. The testes, scrotum, and penis enlarge, and the testes begin to produce sperm cells. Sometimes there is a build up of sperm and fluid (semen) which may be released during sleep. This is called a "**wet dream**" or nocturnal emission and it is a normal occurrence during adolescence.

Some males may be concerned about the difference in appearance of the circumcised or uncircumcised penis. **Circumcision** is a minor operation in which the foreskin of the penis is surgically removed for religious or hygenic purposes. Today, there is a difference of opinion as to the need for circumcision.

Accompanying the various changes in the body is the growth of new body hair. Pubic hair grows around the genitals and, about two years later, hair begins to appear on the face and under the arms. Facial hair first appears as "fuzz" on the upper lip; a beard will develop two or three years later. By age 17, only 50% of males have a beard. Hair on the chest may not start to grow until the age of 19 or 20. The amount of body hair that grows varies from individual to individual.

Breast enlargement may also occur at this time, creating considerable embarrassment for many boys. It is likely caused by small amounts of female sex hormones that are produced by the testes. About 80% of all boys experience this situation during the adolescent years. It is a temporary condition and will disappear.

Physical Changes in Girls

During adolescence, girls grow about 15 cm and gain about 15 kg. They not only change in height and mass during adolescence, they begin to change in shape as well. Sex hormones promote the gradual growth of fatty and glandular tissue in the breasts, and the hips and buttocks become more rounded, creating contours that are different from that of the male. This increase in fatty tissue may cause a temporary increase in mass. In most cases, the extra mass will disappear in a short time.

In the early stages of growth, it is common for one breast to develop faster than another. In fact, many mature women have breasts of unequal size. Shortly after the breasts begin to develop, pubic hair appears around the genital area. Hair

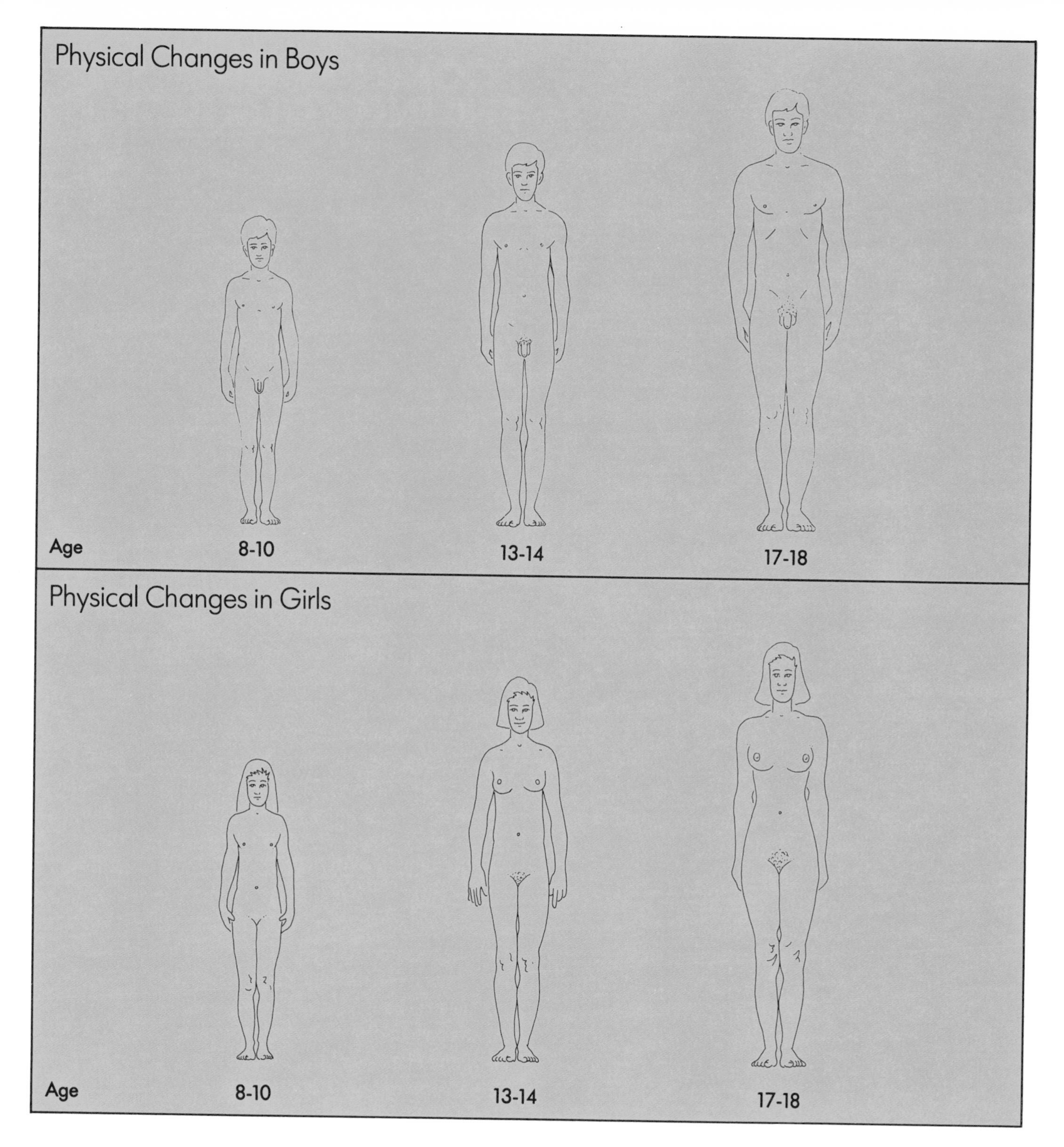
Physical Changes in Boys
Age
8-10
13-14
17-18
Physical Changes in Girls
Age
8-10
13-14
17-18

grows under the arms about two years later. The question of shaving the legs and under the arms is a personal one and varies from culture to culture.

There are other physical changes taking place during adolescence that result in a mature female body. Some of the changes occurring that are not so readily apparent to the eye include: a thickening of the walls of the vagina, a rapid growth of the uterus (which doubles in size) and a widening of the pelvis. A slight white discharge from the vagina is quite common in the mature female. This is a natural cleaning process.

The beginning of menstruation marks an important stage in a girl's life. Menstruation starts about two years after the breasts begin to develop, and indicates that the ovaries are beginning to mature and release ova. (See the discussion of the female reproductive system on p. 112.) Menstruation may last from 1 to 8 days but 3 to 5 days is the average length of time.

Because each girl is physically different, her body will respond to menstruation in its own way. Some girls experience very little discomfort at this time. Other girls may find that their periods are irregular, particularly when they first start. Painful swelling of the breasts and cramps are common. Exercise or a hot bath often will release tension and pain. Menstruation is a normal part of life and there is no need to restrict activities because of it. With convenient sanitary products available today, a girl can engage in a full range of activities, including swimming and other sports.

LOOKING AND FEELING YOUR BEST

Do you spend a lot of time looking in the mirror worrying about your appearance? You may feel that you look awkward and unco-ordinated. Different parts of your body sometimes grow at different rates. In fact, your growth will probably only finish about the age of eighteen. Until then, you may feel self-conscious with adults and peers. However, if you ask your friends, you will likely find that many of them feel this way as well.

If you are concerned about your physical attractiveness, consider what you can do about it. Particular worries at this time might be your complexion, your hair, and body odour. Hormonal change may cause your hair and skin to become oilier than usual. If so, you will want to wash your hair more often. If you have skin problems like pimples and blackheads, you should keep the skin clean by washing it at least twice a day with soap and water. **Acne**, which is a severe case of pimples and blackheads, is usually temporary and will clear up when the hormones in your body stabilize. However, if this condition makes you feel very uncomfortable you should consult a doctor.

Your perspiration, which was previously odourless, now has a distinct smell, especially under your arms. Having a daily bath, using a deodorant, taking a shower after strenuous exercise, and changing your clothes regularly will help to prevent body odour. However, it is felt girls should avoid using feminine hygiene sprays because they may cause vaginal problems. Soap and water are just as effective and are harmless to the body.

Adolescence can be a time of intense feelings. The additional amounts of male and female hormones being produced at this time may quickly change your emotional state, as well as your physical. One moment you may be quite happy, the next you may feel depressed. You may become irritated or cry easily without understanding why. You can feel very energetic one day, and exhausted the next. Life seems so much more complicated than it was before.

When you are depressed, try to get out and do something — see a movie, go jogging or roller-skating — do something that takes your mind off yourself. Sometimes, you may feel like having a good cry, talking to a close friend or being alone to sort out your feelings. Eventually, your body will adjust to hormonal change and your mood swings will gradually become fewer and shorter. You will also become better acquainted with your emotions and more comfortable with methods of dealing with them. While adolescence is often a trying time of your life, it can also bring new experiences, deeper feelings, and a new sense of who you are.

If you are concerned about your physical attractiveness, consider what you can do about it.

YOU AND YOUR RELATIONSHIPS

Up until now, you have been very dependent on adults, particularly your parents. They have been a source of almost all your necessities, from food and shelter to love and approval. Your parents may still regard you as a child because you are still growing. However, as you mature, you will probably want to begin making some decisions for yourself. You may find yourself disagreeing with your parents, particularly over the way you behave.

How do you solve disagreements? Do you talk to your parents about what is important to you or do you become angry and resentful? In order to earn respect for your opinions, you have to be prepared to respect those of others.

As you mature, you begin to decide what is important to you in life. Your values are often the same as those of your parents, but sometimes they are different. When your ideas differ, try to recognize that your parents' values have come out of their experience and that they want to give you the benefit of this experience. By talking over your thoughts with your parents and adult friends in a reasonable way, you may bring about a greater mutual understanding. You may also see more clearly exactly what your values are.

If you can demonstrate responsible behaviour, the adults in your life will develop a feeling of trust in you. When they trust you, they will feel that you are ready for more independent decisions. They will be more comfortable in allowing

DEAR SANDY

My parents have to be the worst people to get along with. They are always ordering me around. It seems I can hardly ever decide for myself what I'm going to do. They tell me when to go to bed, when I have to be home, when to do my homework, sometimes even what to wear. I'm really sick of it. Sometimes I get so frustrated and angry with them I just want to leave home.

The other night I was over at my friend's house and I was supposed to be home at 21:30. Well, I missed the bus that would have got me home on time. My friend and I started talking and I missed the next bus too. Anyway I got home at 23:00 and now my mother has grounded me for a month. I think I'm old enough to decide when I should get home.

Answer

You are growing up and it is understandable that you want to make some decisions for yourself. You should sit down with your parents and discuss your feelings when you are calm and not angry.

You look at your parents' demands as a restriction on your freedom but try to understand that they worry about you. It is up to you to prove that you can make sensible decisions and that you can be considerate of other people.

Your mother was probably very worried when you didn't come home on time. A telephone call would have assured her that you were all right and she might not have given you such a harsh punishment.

you to go on special trips, stay out late on special occasions, or buy your own clothes.

Feelings Toward Friends

At times, it may seem that only your friends understand you. You share activities with them, complain to them, and have secrets with them. Through your friends you find out more about yourself and the world around you. You may spend a lot of time with your friends, especially those of the same sex. In fact, some people your age spend so much time with their friends they think of them as family.

Do you worry about not being part of a group? Most people want to be accepted socially, but making new friends may not always be easy for everyone. What can you do to be a person others like to be with? Find yourself some activities or hobbies that really appeal to you. You will be a more attractive person because you will have a range of interests and something to talk about. Take care of your physical appearance. Review the programs to improve fitness and nutrition and to control body mass discussed in earlier chapters.

Being a member of a group can give you companionship, but friends sometimes pressure you into doing things you do not want to do. You should remember that behaviour is a series of choices, and that you have to choose a course of action that is right for you, and responsible towards others. This can be very difficult when

DEAR SANDY

I am in a new school this year and I don't have any friends here. Making friends has always been hard for me because I'm pretty shy. I can never think of what to say to people I don't know.

I feel so sad and lonely and I don't know what to do about it.

Answer

Adjusting to a new school can be a difficult and lonely experience, especially if you are a shy person. What you have to do is find some people who might be like you. If you have a special interest like music, or stamps, or photography, you could join a school club that centres on that interest. Even if you have no experience in an area, but think you might like to find out about it, you could join a school club. It is easier to make friends with people in a small group than in a large one. If your community has a recreation centre, you might find an activity there that interests you. You could also offer to help one of your classmates with school work or ask for help yourself. Shyness is something that many people experience but it can be overcome in time.

everyone else seems to be doing something you feel is wrong. Being part of the group is important, but so is maintaining your self-respect.

Feelings About the Opposite Sex

Boys and girls usually become more interested in each other sometime during their adolescent years. At first, when you want to approach a member of the opposite sex, you may feel shy and uncertain of yourself. You should keep in mind that the other person is very likely feeling just as shy and uncertain. If you ask a person for a date and are refused, do not look on it as the end of your social life. People have their own reasons for refusing which may not necessarily reflect on you. They may feel they would not know how to act on a date or what to say. They may be dating someone else. You may also find yourself turning down dates on occasion. There is nothing wrong with you if you do not start dating at the same time as your friends, or do not want to date. People who are shy often prefer to be with a group of people.

Boys and girls often express their feelings toward each other by "flirting," joking, or maybe just staring. This is often a way of saying "I like you" or "I am interested in you." As teenagers get to know each other better, they often share their feelings through touching, hand-holding, hugging, and kissing. In a close relationship, it is

DEAR SANDY

There is this girl in my class I really like but I don't think she likes me. I would like to get to know her better but I'm scared she will put me down. I spend so much time thinking about her it is driving me crazy. What can I do?

Answer

If you really want to get to know this girl better, you should develop a plan of action instead of daydreaming. Find out what she is interested in. Maybe the same things interest you. At any rate, knowing what she likes will give you something to talk about. If you are too afraid to approach her directly get to know some of her friends. That way you can join in a conversation with her and get to know her more easily. You have to make her aware of you and give her a chance to like you too.

You should also develop your own interests. If you have something worthwhile to talk about, you will be a more interesting person.

important for you to understand the expectations of the other person. Some people might want companionship, security, love; others might want only to satisfy their own personal needs. Often, the only way to find out what the other person expects, is to ask. It can be difficult to talk about your feelings, particularly if you are afraid of being rejected. However, relationships that last and grow are those in which people can be honest with one another. A good relationship is one in which you maintain your self-respect and your respect for the other person.

If a person becomes involved in an intimate physical relationship, he or she must be prepared to understand the possible risks involved. Both partners must face the chances of pregnancy. People sometimes give excuses for not thinking clearly about this subject. They say things like "I'm too embarrassed to talk about it," "It isn't romantic," "It couldn't happen to me," or "It's the other person's responsibility." The fact is that pregnancy can occur the first time a person is sexually involved, or any time afterwards, if protection is not used. Some methods of conception control are reasonably effective if used properly. However, the only sure way of preventing pregnancy is abstinence.

Pregnancy at an early age can be a serious complication for young people in the process of planning their lives. It may make them increasingly dependent on their parents at a time when they may want to be independent. It may also interfere with their schooling and make new demands on their time. The young mother has to adjust to the physical discomforts of pregnancy and to the prospects of caring for a baby. The young father may be concerned about his role and the responsibility of being a parent. Both may worry about how the pregnancy will affect their relationship and their future life. They may discover that they have to sacrifice some of their own interests and ambitions in order to provide their child with the constant loving care and continual attention it requires. Pregnancy at any age requires people to accept responsibility for others. Young people who have had little experience in making major life decisions are often unprepared for the changes that pregnancy can bring.

BEING FEMALE AND MALE

Though your sex is determined at the moment of conception, how you learn to be female or male is a complex process. The most obvious aspects of male or female behaviour are acquired at an early age. As a young child, you become aware of the physical differences between males and females and you observe various roles within your own family. Your parents may also have certain expectations of you. Girls and boys, for example, are often dressed in different ways and encouraged to have different interests.

Outside your home, you will also be exposed to social attitudes toward male and female behaviour. Relatives, friends, and classmates may expect you to behave in certain ways depending on your sex. Television programs, magazines, films, and advertising also express definite attitudes toward male and female roles through the ways in which they depict men and women. Advertising, in particular, tries to appeal to "masculine" and "feminine" needs.

You may sometimes ask yourself why girls are expected to behave in one way and boys another. The traditional view of men and women is that their responsibilities are determined by their sex. In the past, men were considered to be more capable of earning a living and providing for a family. They held the positions of authority in society. Women were thought to be better suited to raising children because they gave birth. They were regarded as generally not competent to make decisions outside the home. In exchange for protection and support, women were expected to obey their husbands' wishes.

During this century, the traditional views of male and female roles have been changing. Studies in human behaviour have shown that men and women have similar needs and abilities. As a result, attitudes toward the traditional tasks of men and women are altering. As well, new technology has created new job opportunities for both sexes. Because there are many jobs available now that do not require physical strength, women can find work outside the home. Technology has also created effective conception control so that families can plan the arrival of children. Since more women have paying jobs, husbands and children are taking more responsibility at home.

Attitudes toward domestic tasks are changing as well. Men are concerned about playing a more important role in raising their children. They want their children to know them as caring parents. Men are also undertaking tasks formerly thought to be women's work: cooking, washing and ironing, vacuuming, and putting the children to bed. Similarly, women are now doing household jobs that have been considered men's work: shovelling snow, taking out the garbage, repairing appliances, and controlling the finances. Single parents often have to accept a wide range of responsibilities and ask their children for extra help.

Non-traditional jobs are attracting both women and men.

Males and females are undertaking non-traditional tasks.

Even though females and males are doing the same sorts of jobs at home and in the work place, many people still feel that they should play different roles when they socialize together. Traditionally, males have made the first formal move when they have become interested in a female. In the past, a young man might have asked a girl's parents if he could visit. Even today, many boys think that they must be the one to ask a girl out. Many girls, as well, feel that the boy should ask for a date.

Although many young people feel most comfortable following traditional social practices,

there are others who do not think it fair that the boy should always ask the girl, decide on the place and pay for the entertainment. Now, more girls are asking out boys, paying for the date, or splitting the cost. They often phone boys just to talk.

When you care for someone, you may have difficulty knowing how to express your feelings. Traditionally, females were expected to express love, unhappiness, or fear openly. Males, in contrast, were supposed to control their emotions and act bravely, even in difficult circumstances. However, today these expectations are changing as well. Many people feel it is better to express emotions honestly rather than to play roles. Females feel freer to show emotions such as disapproval or anger and males feel freer to show emotions such as unhappiness and tenderness.

Trying to decide how to behave as a female or male can be puzzling, particularly when many people have different attitudes to the subject. You will have to decide for yourself what behaviour makes you most comfortable. However, as you consider your own needs and rights, be sure to think about those of other people as well. Learning to find a balance between your own needs and those of other people is an essential part of growing up.

LEARNING ABOUT ALCOHOL

Drinking alcoholic beverages is a part of North American culture and for many people it is an essential ingredient in any social event. Most drinkers consume alcohol in moderation, and they drink for a variety of reasons. They may find that a drink relaxes them after a hard working day or makes them feel at ease in social situations. Many people enjoy an alcoholic beverage with a meal or as part of a family gathering or religious celebration. There are also people who choose not to drink. They do so for such reasons as religious beliefs, possible damage to their health, fear of addiction, or simply a dislike of the taste.

Because alcoholic beverages are often part of social occasions, you may already have been offered a drink. Choosing whether to drink or how much to drink are personal decisions you may have to make during your adolescent years.

Sometimes people find themselves drinking when they do not really want to. They may drink in order to be accepted by others. People of all ages experience this kind of pressure, but teen-agers often feel it very strongly because being accepted by friends their own age is very important at this stage of their lives.

Other sorts of pressures also cause young people to drink. Having a drink may seem to be a good way to forget about problems for a while. It may seem easier to make friends after having a few drinks. Difficulties at home or at school may not seem so serious. Lack of money may seem less of a worry. Often drinking is used to escape boredom and the feeling that there is nothing to do. However, people sometimes forget that drinking does not solve their problems; in fact, it may create new ones if they drink excessively.

Effects of Alcohol on the Body

The term "alcohol" is applied to a number of chemical compounds. **Methyl alcohol** is used in hair tonic and windshield washer fluid, and **isopropyl alcohol** (rubbing alcohol) is used to reduce fevers and to cleanse wounds. Both of these alcohols are poisonous if taken internally. The alcohol contained in alcoholic beverages is called **ethyl alcohol**.

There are three main types of alcoholic drink: beer, wine, and liquor or spirits. The production of these drinks involves **fermentation**, a process by which yeast changes the sugar in plant substances into carbon dioxide and alcohol. Beer and liquors are made mainly from grains and wine is made from fruit.

Alcohol has an effect on many systems in the body. When it is taken in, it is absorbed into the bloodstream and circulates to all parts of the body. About 20% of the alcohol is absorbed directly from the stomach into the bloodstream. The other 80% moves quickly or slowly into the small intestine, depending on the amount of food in the stomach. If there is no food in the stomach, the alcohol moves quickly into the small intestine

TRUE OR FALSE?

1. Alcohol cures snakebite.
2. Hot coffee or a cold shower helps to sober up a person who is drunk.
3. Very few women become alcoholics.
4. Alcoholics are generally people on unemployment insurance.
5. You cannot become an alcoholic if you only drink beer.
6. Drinking a little alcohol will always improve your physical skills.
7. You can only become an alcoholic over the age of 40.
8. Alcohol improves fading eyesight.

(Answers to all of the above are false)

Alcohol Content of Beverages

Drink	Example	% Alcohol
Beer	ale	about 5%
Wine	red table wine	about 12%
Liquor (distilled)	rye whiskey	about 40%
Liqueurs	creme de menthe	10%-40%

where it is rapidly absorbed into the bloodstream. A person may almost immediately feel light-headed or intoxicated. If there is food in the stomach, the **pyloric valve** between the stomach and intestine closes so that the process of digestion can begin. This means that 80% of the alcohol taken in will be released slowly into the small intestines. From there it will be absorbed into the bloodstream.

The alcohol in the bloodstream causes the blood vessels to dilate and the flow of blood to increase. As a result, the skin becomes warmer and red in colour and the person may actually begin to perspire. Even the eyes may turn red and become bloodshot.

Alcohol is also a drug that affects the brain and all areas that the brain controls. Because it slows down part of the brain it is called a **depressant**. Some people choose to use small amounts of alcohol to relax themselves. In fact, life insurance statistics show that a person who drinks small amounts of alcohol is likely to live longer than a person who does not drink at all. Clearly then, it is a drug that can have a beneficial effect on the body if used in moderation. However, excessive drinking causes loss of inhibitions and of motor control, slurred speech, and eventually unconsciousness.

Some alcohol is eliminated through the lungs in breathing. However, most alcohol remains in the bloodstream until the liver has a chance to break it down. The average healthy liver converts 15 mL of alcohol per hour into water, **acetic acid** (the acid in vinegar), carbon dioxide, and heat and/or energy. Because of the increase in water, urination is more frequent. The rate of breakdown is determined only by the size and condition of the liver. Therefore, coffee, walks in the fresh air, and showers will not help in eliminating alcohol from the body.

A **hangover** usually occurs the day after a number of alcoholic drinks have been consumed. The degree of hangover depends on the personality, the amount drunk, and the mood of the drinker. It usually produces a headache, extreme thirst, dizziness, and an upset stomach.

Clearly, the more alcohol a person drinks and the more quickly he or she consumes it, the higher the degree of **intoxication**. Alcoholic drinks that are taken rapidly increase the blood alcohol level, without giving the liver a chance to break it down and eliminate it. The contents of a drink have an effect on the speed and degree of intoxication. Mixed drinks have varying effects. A drink containing milk or cream, which is high in protein, closes the stomach for a longer period of time. Water in a drink dilutes the alcohol. The gas in carbonated drinks increases the speed with which alcohol is absorbed into the blood. Straight liquor on an empty stomach is absorbed quickly, with a greater immediate effect.

Body size will also determine the effect of alcohol on a person because the alcohol is diluted by the blood. The larger a body the person has, the more blood the person has and the more diluted the alcohol becomes. For example, a person whose mass is 45 kg will have a blood alcohol level of about 0.09% (illegal for driving) after drinking three drinks in 1 h. A 90 kg person will have a blood level of 0.04% (legal for driving) after drinking the identical three drinks in 1 h. The greater the dilution of alcohol, the less effect it has on the brain and other parts of the body.

When a person is tired, alcohol may have a greater effect. During illness, the body is usually suffering fatigue in its fight to overcome a germ or virus. Cold pills, **tranquillizers**, codeine (used as a cough medicine) or **sedatives** (sleeping pills), and even **marijuana** may greatly increase the effects of alcohol on the body.

Most doctors agree that the consumption of large quantities of alcohol is a factor contributing to liver ailments. As the rate of consumption of

WHY DO THEY DRINK?

Suggest why the following people are drinking:

1. Your school has a rule against drinking and yet Tom keeps a bottle in his locker and sneaks out between periods to have a drink.
2. Spiro has had a few drinks when he comes to pick up his date.
3. Kae asks two of her classmates over to her house after school to have a few drinks from her parent's liquor cabinet while they are away.

alcohol increases, so do the number of related diseases. A disease such as **cirrhosis** often progresses slowly, taking 15 to 20 years to develop. The damage is permanent and the disease has no cure. However, if a person stops drinking heavily, further damage can be avoided.

If you choose to drink you have a responsibility to yourself and to others. Responsibility to yourself includes:

- drinking only if you want to
- drinking in moderation and knowing how you respond to alcohol
- choosing friends who will not pressure you to drink if you do not want to
- not combining drinking with other drugs
- not drinking and driving.

It is sometimes easier to make responsible decisions for yourself than to control the behaviour of others. If people around you are drinking excessively what should you do? First of all, you should not provide alcohol for a person who is already drunk. You should also try to prevent someone who has been drinking heavily from driving. If someone you know well appears to be increasingly reliant on alcohol, encourage him or her to seek professional help. Physicians, school counsellors, clergy, and community clinics can offer advice to problem drinkers. If the person is an alcoholic, organizations such as Alcoholics Anonymous (AA), Al-Anon, and Alateen as well as a number of rehabilitation centres will offer counselling and support.

DECIDING ABOUT ALCOHOL

To help you to make important and difficult decisions on alcohol use ask yourself the following questions:

What choices do I have?
What do I know?
What do I value?
What are my feelings?
How would other people feel?
What might happen?

Try this process for making decisions when considering the consequences of the following actions:

1. You are under the legal age for drinking and some friends ask you to go drinking with them.
2. Some of your friends challenge you to a "chug-a-lug" contest.
3. An acquaintance offers you some unidentified pills to take, while the two of you are drinking. He tells you that you will enjoy the effect.
4. You know that your best friend drinks too much but he or she will not admit it.
5. You are leaving a party and are offered a ride home by a good friend who is drunk.
6. Some of your classmates have decided to take some beer with them on a school canoe trip. The teacher has asked that no alcohol be brought on the trip.

MAKING CHOICES — A LIFETIME DEMAND

As an adolescent and as an adult, you will often have to make choices about the direction of your life. Some of those decisions will be wise and others will be foolish. Some decisions you make as a young person will hold for the rest of your life. Others that were right for you as an adolescent may not be appropriate when you are an adult. In order to make decisions that will benefit you, it is important to know your feelings and your strengths and weaknesses. By understanding your own needs you will be better able to build a happy, secure place for yourself in the world.

FOR REVIEW

Key Ideas

- Adolescence is a period in your life when you undergo major physical and emotional changes.
- Hormones are responsible for the physical and emotional changes boys and girls experience during adolescence.
- During adolescence your relationships with parents and friends may change.
- Most boys and girls develop an interest in the opposite sex during adolescence.
- Learning to be male and female is a complex process that begins during childhood and continues through adolescence.
- Drinking alcoholic beverages is a part of our culture.
- Alcohol affects many parts of the body including the brain, liver, stomach, and blood vessels.
- You should behave responsibly if you choose to drink.

Questions and Activities

1. Describe some of the changes that occur in girls and boys at puberty.
2. Describe some of the ways you can show another person you like him or her.
3. What effect does alcohol have on the brain?
4. How can you behave responsibly in a situation where people are drinking excessively?
5. Debate the following topics:
   a. Some people are born with the ability to make friends.
   b. Beauty and brains count most in winning friends.
   c. Having plenty of spending money is a sure way of making friends.
   d. Wearing the latest fashions is the best way of gaining popularity.
6. List six traits that you think are important in a friend. Give yourself a rating between one and three for each one of the traits you have listed. A rating of three indicates this trait appears strongly in you. Do you think you make a good friend?
7. List the things that usually make you worry. Compile a master list with other students and discuss ways of overcoming these problems.
8. Survey 10 boys and 10 girls at school on the following questions: "Should girls ask boys for a date?" "Should a girl phone a boy regularly?" Present your findings to the rest of the class.
9. How would you answer this letter if you were the editor of "Youth Help," a write-in column for your local newspaper.

   I am a girl (boy) 13 years old. I'm considered good looking but I'm shy. When a boy (girl) starts a conversation with me, I can't think of anything to say. I need some ideas on how to make conversation.
10. Write a letter yourself to "Youth Help" describing a problem you are worried about. Exchange letters with your classmates and write appropriate answers.
11. Develop a list of activities you engage in that might be difficult for you to abstain from. Examples might be: using salt and/or sugar, using the telephone, drinking soda pop, or watching television. Select one activity and try to abstain from it for 4 days. Write a brief report on this experiment. Consider: *a.* your feelings—anger, boredom, grouchiness, jealousy; *b.* what you have learned about addiction.
12. Make a collection of advertisements for alcohol (at least 10) and analyse them with regard to: devices used to attract you, effect on you, age group directed at.
13. Research and report on the activities of Alateen and the Al-Anon programs for alcoholic abuse.
14. What is the legal age for drinking in your province? Discuss whether this age should be raised or lowered.

Your Body / The Inside Story
Demonstration

CHAPTER SEVEN

A SERIOUS HEALTH PROBLEM

SEXUALLY TRANSMITTED DISEASES

Most people are aware of the fight against heart disease and cancer, two of the great health concerns of our day. However, few know much about a group of diseases that is increasing at an alarming rate here in Canada and throughout the world: sexually transmitted diseases or STD. Five of the most common STD are **syphilis, gonorrhea, herpes genitalis, non-gonococcal urethritis** (NGU), and **vaginitis**.

Each year in Canada there are over 50 000 reported cases of gonorrhea alone. Canadian authorities have stated that for each case of STD reported, there are 2 or 3 cases that go unreported. Thus, while STD statistics are alarming enough, they only hint at the problem. To get a clearer picture, look at the circlegraph. STD were responsible for over 55% of all the communicable diseases reported to Statistics Canada in the early 1980s. Another alarming fact is that half of the STD reported involved young people between the ages of 15 and 25 years.

Why Are STD so Common?

Unfortunately, people who will freely admit to having measles, may feel embarrassed about having STD since these diseases are transmitted only by sexual contact. As well, the symptoms of STD are often not present or disappear quickly only to reappear later in a more serious form. As a result, infected people may not report the disease and obtain treatment. They may then pass it to others.

The problem of STD is a baffling one. Modern medicine has known for a long time how the diseases spread and how to treat them. In fact, STD could be virtually eliminated as were the widespread diseases of polio, typhoid fever, and the bubonic plague in earlier times. However, until people understand the seriousness of these diseases, they will continue in epidemic proportions and cause unnecessary suffering.

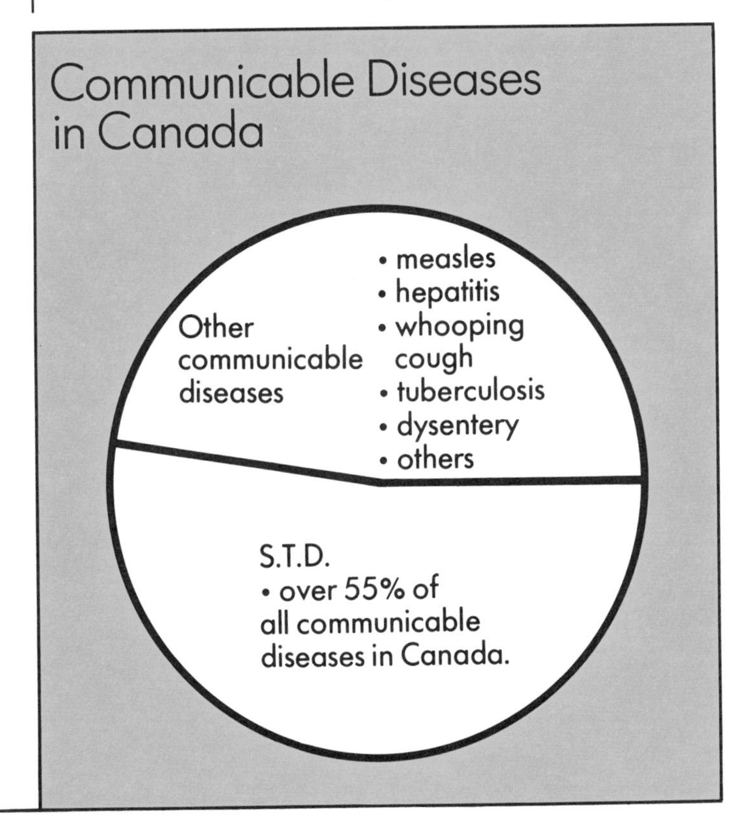

Talking to someone who knows the facts is important.

WHY LEARN ABOUT STD?

- To avoid STD.
- To recognize signs and symptoms.
- To help others.
- To know places for treatment.
- To be aware of the dangers of STD.
- To protect unborn children.
- To prevent the spread of STD.
- To learn how common STD are.
- To learn types of treatment.
- To know that most STD can be treated.

SOME TYPES OF SEXUALLY TRANSMITTED DISEASE

Syphilis

Syphilis is the most dangerous of the STD. If untreated, it can lead to insanity, paralysis, blindness, heart disease, and even death. It can also severely affect unborn babies because it can be transmitted through the placenta.

The bacteria that cause syphilis are passed on by physical contact with an infected person. They enter the body through the mucous membranes, which are the soft, moist tissues that line the body exits. They can also enter the body through any skin surface that is cut or broken. Within hours they reach the bloodstream and are carried to all parts of the body.

There are 5 stages of syphilis: incubation, primary syphilis, secondary syphilis, latent syphilis, and late syphilis. Each has a different set of symptoms, although in many cases the symptoms are hidden or do not appear.

The incubation stage refers to the time between contact and the appearance of symptoms. During this time there are no signs or symptoms of the disease. However, the germs are rapidly multiplying every 30 to 33 h and later are carried to all parts of the body by the blood and **lymph systems**. During this stage the person is infected (has the disease), but is not infectious (cannot pass the disease on).

During the primary stage of syphilis, a lesion or **chancre** (pronounced shang-ker) appears where the spirochete entered. The chancre is

FACTS EVERYONE SHOULD KNOW ABOUT STD.

1. NGU (Non-Gonococcal Urethritis) is the most common STD in Canada.
2. Each STD is a different disease.
3. STD are spread only through direct physical contact with infected people.
4. A person can have more than one STD at the same time.
5. So far, no effective vaccine has been discovered to provide immunity to any of the diseases.
6. A person could have STD and not know it. The only way to be sure is to be checked by a doctor.
7. Most STD can be cured but the damage already done cannot be reversed.
8. People of either sex and any age can contact STD.
9. The fact that the symptoms go away does not mean that STD are cured.
10. There is no cure for Herpes Genitalis

almost always painless and feels like a button under the skin surface. It is usually hard and crusty but it can be soft. While it is harmless looking, it is teeming with spirochetes and is highly infectious. In the majority of males, it appears in the genital region. In the female, the chancre may appear on the exterior genitals but more often appears on the cervix where it often goes undetected. The chancre can also appear on the tongue, lips, finger, anus, and breast of both males and females. There may also be more than one. In some cases the chancre does not appear at all, yet the person still has syphilis. The dangerous aspect of this stage is that the chancre will disappear in 2 to 5 weeks, even if it is untreated. This does not mean that the disease has been eliminated, but rather that it has entered a different stage.

The second stage of syphilis occurs from 6 weeks to 6 months after initial contact. It can be an infectious stage when it produces an open rash or open sores filled with bacteria. Individuals show a variety of symptoms which may appear alone, or in groups, and may be mild or severe. Many people experience a low fever and feel unwell. Frequently there is a swelling of the various lymph glands and multiple sores and ulcers in the mouth and genital areas. Often a rash may appear on the skin and a person may suffer from a sore throat and sore joints. Occasionally, patches of hair may fall out.

The organism which causes syphilis is a spirochete that is shaped like a cork screw.

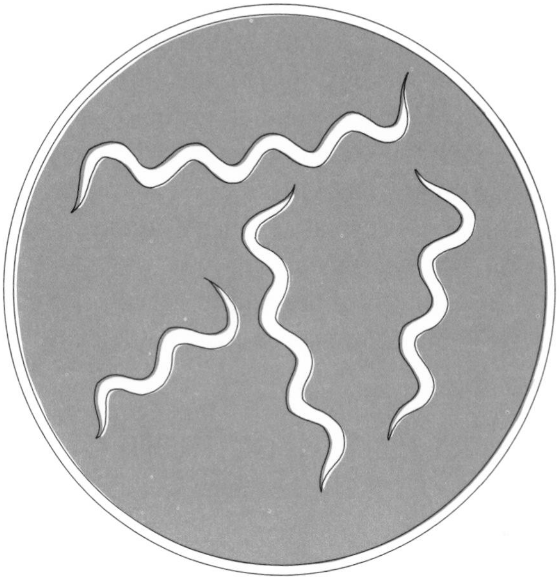

It is easy to understand why syphilis is often not recognized as all these symptoms could easily be signs of something else such as the flu. As with primary syphilis, the symptoms will eventually disappear even if they are untreated. However, they may reappear from time to time for up to 2 years.

During the latent or hidden stage, there are no symptoms at all, and the person with the disease feels healthy. Throughout this period, which can last from 5 to 20 years, the germs are constantly multiplying and attacking various parts including the brain, the heart, and spinal cord. Since no chancres are present, the disease is not infectious at this stage.

Late syphilis is the final and the most severe stage of the disease. A third of those who have untreated syphilis will develop serious symptoms in later years. It may take 10 to 20 years for the damage to appear but when it does, it may be fatal. The disease can attack many organs. Syphilis of the heart can result in heart attacks and death. Syphilis of the central nervous system can destroy important nerve centres and cause insanity, blindness, or paralysis.

Detection and Treatment of Syphilis

Only qualified medical personnel are trained to diagnose syphilis. Special blood tests are used to detect antibodies produced by the body to fight syphilis.

Penicillin in the proper dosages is the most appropriate treatment for this disease and it is very effective. If a person is allergic to penicillin or is pregnant, other suitable **antibiotics** are used.

A very serious aspect of the disease is the potential effect it can have on unborn babies. Syphilis is passed on from the infected mother to the fetus through the placenta. It can cause deafness, blindness, mental retardation, and in some cases, even death. The damage from syphilis to the newborn ordinarily occurs after the fourth month of pregnancy. Treatment of the mother with penicillin is usually very effective in the first 4 months. For this reason some provinces require blood tests from all pregnant women.

PRE-MARITAL BLOOD TESTS

One measure to detect and control syphilis is to give pre-marital blood tests. In Canada, only Alberta, Manitoba, Saskatchewan, and Prince Edward Island require this. In one year in the U.S.A., pre-marital tests in 27 states uncovered 12 250 cases of syphilis. One out of every 81 marriage applicants had laboratory evidence of syphilis. If blood tests were required, people who have syphilis could be treated immediately to prevent the spread of the disease to their partner or future offspring.

Gonorrhea

The bacteria which cause gonorrhea enter the body through mucous membranes such as those found in the urethra and vagina. Gonorrhea, therefore, is transmitted almost always by sexual contact and if untreated spreads upward along the genital tract. This disease affects men and women in different ways because of their anatomical differences. In a woman, the disease moves up the vagina to the uterus, Fallopian tubes, and ovaries. These organs can become infected and inflamed, causing extensive damage to the reproductive system. If the damage is extensive, the woman will not be able to have children, that is, she becomes sterile. In a man, the infection can spread up the urethra to the prostate gland, the vas deferens, and testes, causing sterility. If untreated, gonorrhea can also cause a narrowing of the urethra, making urination painful. A severe infection may also result in **arthritis** and organ damage.

The organism responsible for gonorrhea is called a gonococcus and is shaped like a coffee bean.

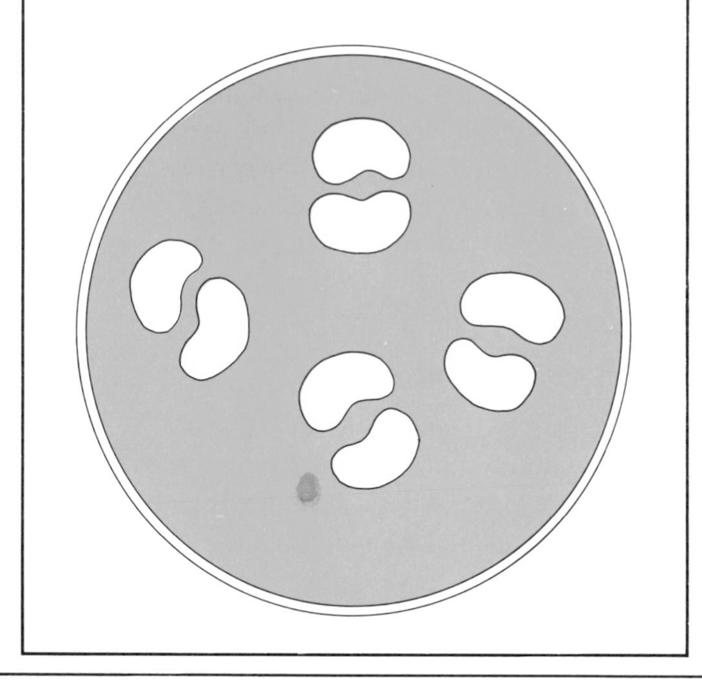

Once the **gonococcus** bacteria are in the body, the incubation period is very short. The gonococci divide and multiply quickly and symptoms appear in 3 to 7 days. In males, the gonococci attack the membranes of the urethra causing an infection called urethritis. This usually results in frequent, painful urination and a thick yellow discharge from the penis. Females frequently have no symptoms at all, though they may occasionally experience a mild burning sensation urinating, and a vaginal discharge. Although 80% of females and 15% of males may have no symptoms at all, they are still capable of spreading the infection.

Detection and Treatment of Gonorrhea

Gonorrhea must be diagnosed by a qualified doctor. To detect the disease, a smear is made of the discharge and examined under a microscope. Penicillin in adequate amounts is the usual treatment; however, other antibiotics have also been effective.

A pregnant woman, infected with gonorrhea, can transmit the disease to the eyes of her newborn baby as it descends the birth canal. Because of this possibility, all hospitals in Canada are required to treat the eyes of newborn babies with **silver nitrate** or penicillin.

A NEW PENICILLIN-RESISTANT STD

In October 1976, the first three cases of gonorrhea totally resistant to penicillin were reported to Canadian federal health authorities. Prior to this, there were some strains known to be difficult to control with penicillin but this was the first to be totally resistant.

This dangerous new strain points out the very serious results when a disease is out of control. As more and more people contract the disease, traditional methods of treatment become increasingly less effective.

Herpes Genitalis

Herpes genitalis is passed on by intimate skin to skin contact. However, unlike gonorrhea and syphilis, it is not caused by bacteria; it results from a virus similar to the virus that causes cold sores. This disease may cause inflammation of the brain (encephalitis) and may make women more susceptible to cancer of the cervix. The presence of this virus in the bloodstream of a pregnant woman during the first three months of pregnancy will affect the developing baby and may cause miscarriage. The virus can also be transmitted to a baby as it passes through the birth canal. It may cause encephalitis in the baby. There is no drug that can cure herpes genitalis. Once a person is infected, sores may continue to recur.

Symptoms appear 2 to 21 days after the virus enters the body. The first signs that appear are itching and irritation in the genital regions, which quickly change to an intense burning. In a few days, a group of water-like blisters appear on the genitals. A few days later, the blisters become sores and the tissue in this area swells and becomes quite painful. The sores will last for about 10 days and heal themselves if they have not become infected with bacteria. Because there is a virus in the blood stream there may be a low fever, swollen glands, and other "flu-like" symptoms. In some cases, the symptoms will disappear, although the virus is still present in the cells of the skin. Periodically it may cause fresh sores to appear. A person is still contagious during these periods of recurrence.

Detection and Treatment of Herpes Genitalis

This disease is diagnosed in several ways. A doctor will look at the patient; the discharge from the blister or sores will be examined under a microscope; and occasionally, a blood test will be administered.

Though there is no drug to cure herpes genitalis, ointment may be prescribed to relieve pain. The sores should be kept clean and dry to prevent infection. If infection occurs, a doctor may prescribe an antibiotic like penicillin to control it.

Non-Gonococcal Urethritis (NGU)

Non-gonococcal urethritis is not a well-known sexually transmitted disease and yet it is the most widespread of all these diseases. It is thought to be caused by a bacteria that can damage the reproductive organs of both males and females.

In men, the bacteria can lead to blockage of the vas deferens (sperm ducts) resulting in sterility. Women, too, can become sterile if the Fallopian tubes are blocked. Babies born to infected women can develop eye infections and various pneumonia-like infections during early infancy.

The symptoms of NGU which appear 1 to 6 weeks after contact are relatively mild and people often don't seek treatment. The symptoms for men include pain during urination and a clear watery discharge (as opposed to the thick yellow discharge associated with gonorrhea). Some women may have a vaginal discharge but, in most cases, they experience no symptoms at all.

Detection and Treatment of NGU

NGU is difficult to detect since the symptoms may be absent or mistaken for gonorrhea. The disease is not easy to treat either, because it does not respond to penicillin. Other antibiotics have to be used in the treatment of this STD.

Vaginitis

Vaginitis is an inflammation of the vagina which is often indicated by a discharge. There are two common forms of vaginitis that occur in women. One form, called **trichomoniasis**, is caused by a tiny one-celled animal. It is transferred to a female by her male partner, who often has no symptoms of the disease himself. Some women experience no symptoms but others suffer from an irritating greenish-yellow discharge.

Trichomoniasis is diagnosed by examining a drop of the discharge. Several drugs are used to cure this disease. It is also important to treat the male partner at the same time as the female to prevent the infection from being passed back and forth.

The most common form of vaginitis is **vaginal thrush**, a fungus which can affect adolescent girls and grown women. It can occur in females who are not sexually active as well as in those who are. However, males may become infected from contact with an infected female and, as a result, develop urethritis. Women have a slight watery discharge or a heavy one containing white curd-like material. This infection is diagnosed by examining a drop of the discharge. To obtain treatment, a person must see a doctor who will prescribe an antibiotic cream.

PREVENTION AND TREATMENT OF SEXUALLY TRANSMITTED DISEASES

Sexually transmitted diseases are communicable diseases that are transmitted primarily by sexual contact. Therefore, it is natural to assume that the best method to prevent infection is to abstain from sexual activity. If sexual contact does occur there are a number of ways to partially reduce the chance of infection. A condom, used by the male during sexual activity, can be useful in protecting both males and females. Urination and washing with soap and water immediately after sexual contact may help in killing or removing the bacteria. If partial or no protection has been taken, then it is most important to obtain periodic medical checkups. Recognition of signs and symptoms can also help, but it should be remembered that many people, particularly women, have no obvious signs or symptoms. The only sure way of avoiding STD is abstinence from sexual contact.

The symptoms of sexually transmitted diseases are similar to those of other infections particularly in the genital region. It is sometimes difficult to know what the infection is. However, because of the seriousness of these diseases, it is important for people to be diagnosed promptly.

Larger cities often have STD clinics (check under government listings in the telephone book for VD or STD clinics) that are free. Public health departments also offer free medical help. A person may see a doctor privately as well.

A person visiting a clinic will often be given a number when she or he enters. Later, in private, a nurse will record that person's name, address, and telephone number. The nurse will ask if the person wants to get in touch with his or her contacts or whether the clinic should. Any information given at the clinic is kept completely confidential. It is against the law for clinic personnel to reveal any names.

A doctor will examine the person, take blood samples, and do tests for the diseases. In the case of gonorrhea, the analysis may be done in the clinic so that the person will know immediately. The results of tests for syphilis usually take about one week.

Because these diseases are so serious, a person is usually treated even if the disease is only suspected. Males return to the clinic one week after treatment for gonorrhea, females come back for two weeks in a row, and both return after six weeks for a checkup. When a person has been treated for syphilis, he or she should return monthly for three months, after one year, and again after two years.

Timing is an important factor in the diagnosis and treatment of STD. The sooner an infected person receives treatment, the better. In the early stages before serious damage happens, treatment is relatively straightforward. Sexual contacts can also be diagnosed before the disease has advanced. Since regular routine physical checkups will not necessarily reveal STD, anyone engaging in sexual activity should have these tests. It is essential that special tests for STD be requested by sexually active individuals.

Get help if you are unsure about your health.

FOR REVIEW

Key Ideas

- The incidence of STD is increasing rapidly in Canada.
- Syphilis is the most dangerous of the STD.
- Gonorrhea is a very common sexually transmitted disease which can cause sterility.
- Herpes Genitalis is caused by a virus and has no cure.
- NGU is the most widespread of the STD.
- Two common forms of vaginitis occur in women and can be transmitted sexually.
- It is important that STD be treated promptly.
- Special clinics for treating STD exist in all larger cities. These clinics are free.

Questions and Activities

1. What are some reasons for the spread of STD?
2. Why is prompt treatment essential?
3. Research the following aspects of treatment for STD in your community:
   a. location for STD diagnosis and treatment
   b. methods of diagnosis for each STD
   c. methods of treatment for each STD
   d. costs
   e. confidentiality (who is told about the STD).
4. Report on new penicillin-resistant strains of gonorrhea. Indicate the reasons for concern, the diagnosis and treatment, and the possible future development of these types of bacteria.
5. Describe all methods of preventing or reducing the amount of STD. Rank these methods from most effective to least effective. What is the most effective? The least effective method? Why?
6. Write a report on the following:
   a. why STD is more serious for women
   b. why it is so important to reveal contacts (particularly females)
   c. steps that would reduce STD in newborn children.

GLOSSARY

Pronunciation Guide

a	hat, cap	u	cup, butter
ā	age, face	u̇	full, put
ã	care, air	ü	rule, move
ä	barn, far	ū	use, music
e	let, best	ə	represents:
ē	equal, be		a in above, pillar
	y as in pretty		e in taken, under
ėr	term, learn		i in pencil, tapir
i	it, pin		o in lemon, favor
ī	ice, five		u in circus, measure
o	hot, rock		
ō	open, go		
ô	order, door		
oi	oil, voice		
ou	out, loud		

FROM: The Gage Canadian Dictionary, back end paper
Gage Educational Publishing Limited, Toronto, 1973

a bra sion a cut or scrape that occurs on the surface of the skin.

a ce tic ac id (ə sē′tik as′id) a component of vinegar.

ac ne (ak′nē) a skin condition characterized by blackheads and pimples.

ad di tive a substance that may be added to foods during processing to preserve them or make them more attractive.

ad re nal glands (ə drē′nəl glandz) ductless glands located on top of the kidneys which produce androgen sex hormones or androgen, adrenalin and other hormones.

a dren al in (ə dren′əl in) a hormone secreted by the adrenal glands responsible for increasing the heart rate and blood pressure in a stressful situation.

aer o bics (ār ō′biks) activities or exercises which make use of the large muscles and require large quantities of oxygen.

a gil i ty the ability to change the direction and position of your body quickly with control.

al ve o li (al vē′ə lē) tiny air sacs at the end of the bronchioles, where the exchange of oxygen and carbon dioxide takes place in the lungs.

a mi no a cids (ə mē′nō as′idz) complex organic substances that combine to form proteins.

am ni o sent es is (am nē ō sent ēs′is) a test sometimes done on pregnant women to sample the amniotic fluid surrounding the baby. This test can determine the fetus' sex and if it has certain diseases or defects.

am ni ot ic flu id (am nē ot′ik flü′ id) a fluid contained in a sac that protects and cushions the baby in the uterus.

am phet a mines (am fet′a mēns) drugs that can be used as stimulants to reduce the appetite.

an aes thet ic (an is thet′ ik) a drug or process to dull the sensation of pain.

an dro gens (an′drə jənz) hormones secreted by the adrenal glands and by the testes in males, which stimulate growth, and in males, promote the development of the genitals.

an o rex i a ner vos a (an ō reks′ē a nər′ vōs ə) an illness where a person is obsessed with being thin to the extent that he or she becomes undernourished.

an ti bi ot ics (an tē bī ot′ iks) substances produced by organisms which can hinder the growth of or kill other micro-organisms. Penicillin is an example of a drug that is an antibiotic.

a or ta (ā ôr′tə) the major artery carrying oxygen-rich blood from the heart to the body.

ar ter y (är′tər ē) a thick-walled muscular vessel which carries blood from the heart throughout the body.

ar thri tis (är thrī′tis) a condition where a joint or joints are inflamed, making the area swollen and painful and movement difficult.

ar ti fi cial res pir a tion a method of bringing in and expelling air from the lungs of someone who is unable to breathe.

ath er o scle ro sis (ath ər ō sclə rō′sis) a disease associated with cholesterol deposits on the walls of the arteries.

a tri um (ā′trē əm) one of the two upper chambers of the heart.

bac ter i a microscopic, one-celled organisms, capable of dividing by fission, sometimes causing disease, but also performing useful functions.

ba lance the ability to keep the body in a stable position while still or moving.

ba sal me tab o lic rate (bā′səl me tə bo′ lic rāt) the amount of energy, varying from person to person, required to keep the internal systems of the body functioning.

blas to cyst (blas′ tō sist) a stage in the development of a fetus, when the growing ball of cells, with an inner cavity and a group of cells on one side, has become implanted on the wall of the uterus.

blood pres sure a measure of the pressure exerted by the blood on the walls of the blood vessels. This pressure is measured twice to give a full reading; at the moment the heart beats, and when it is at rest.

bond ing the development of emotional attachments between a baby and its parents.

bron chi (brong′ kī) tubes that carry air into the lungs. The windpipe divides into two main bronchi, which in turn divide into several smaller bronchi.

bron chi tis (brong kī′ tis) a respiratory illness that occurs when the bronchi become inflamed.

car bo hy drates (kar bō hī′drāts) the sugars and starches in foods, which are the main supply of energy for the body.

Cae sar e an sec tion (si zār′ē ən sek shən) an operation performed if a baby is too large for the pelvic opening, or the placenta is blocking the passage through the birth canal. The operation consists of cutting through the abdominal wall and the uterus to remove the baby.

caf feine (kaf′ēn) a substance found in coffee, tea, cocoa, and some soft drinks that acts as a stimulant.

cal is then ics (kal is then′iks) rhythmical exercises for the body done with little or no apparatus, to promote flexibility, muscular strength, and to some extent, muscular endurance and cardiorespiratory fitness.

cap il la ries (kap′ə ler ēs) tiny blood vessels that form a mesh between the arteries and the veins.

car cin o gens (kär sin′ə jəns) cancer-causing substances.

car di o res pi ra to ry fit ness (kär dē ō res′ pə rə tô rē fit nəs) involves the health and efficiency of the heart, lungs, and blood vessels.

car ti lage (kär′ tə lij) a tough white gristle which covers the ends of the bones and protects the bones from rubbing against each other.

cer vix (sėr′viks) the base of the uterus where it joins the vagina.

chan cre (shang′ kər) in primary syphilis, a painless lesion or sore on the skin surface located where the bacteria entered the body.

cho les ter ol (kə les′tər ol) a white substance found in animal fats and products, that solidifies at room temperature.

chro mo somes (krō′mə sōms) filaments which carry genetic material, contained in the nucleus of every cell. Normal human cells contain 46 chromosomes.

cil i a (sil′ē ə) hairlike projections attached to special cells which line the Fallopian tubes and the bronchi. The rhythmic beating of the cilia in the Fallopian tubes propels the ovum toward the uterus. Cilia in the bronchi help to expel mucus and particles that have been inhaled.

cir cuit train ing (sėr′kit trān′ing) a method of fitness training where one type of exercise is practised at one location for a period of time, then another type at another location. This type of training improves the fitness of different areas of the body with exercises specific to the area.

cir cu la tor y sys tem (sėr′kyu̇ lə tô rē sis′təm) the system by which the blood circulates through the body, carrying food and oxygen to body cells, and removing the waste products.

cir cum ci sion (sėr kəm sizh′ən) a surgical operation to remove the foreskin of the penis for religious or hygenic reasons.

cir rho sis (sə rō sis) disease of the liver causing degeneration of the liver cells.

col lat er al cir cu la tion (kə lat′ər əl sėr kyū lā′shən) small arteries which allow blood to bypass a blocked artery.

con cep tion (kən sep′shən) the joining together of the ovum and the sperm.

cool—down a period after strenuous activity in which stretching exercises and slow simulation of the activity are done to loosen the muscles and prevent injuries.

co—or din a tion the ability to use your senses, together with your arms or legs, or to use two or more body parts at the same time.

cor o nar y ar ter y (kôr′ə ner ē är′tər ē) one of two elastic walled blood vessels that carry blood from the aorta back to sustain the heart itself.

de pres sant a substance that reduces the functioning of a body organ. Alcohol, for example, reduces the functioning of the brain.

di as tol ic pres sure (dī əs tol′ik presh′ər) a measure of the blood pressure when the heart is at rest. It is the lower of the two readings in a blood pressure reading.

di u ret ic (dī yu̇ ret′ik) a substance or process which increases the volume of urine produced.

ec to morph (ek′tə môrf) a type of body build that has light bones and very little fat.

e jac u la tion (i jak yu lā′shən) the stage in male sexual response when sperm and fluids (semen) move through the vas deferens, prostate gland, urethra, and out the opening of the penis.

e lec tro car di o gram (i lek trō kär′dē ə gram) a tracing made by an instrument which measures the electrical activity of the heart muscle.

em bry o (em′brē ō) the name for the developing baby during the first two months in the uterus.

em phy se ma (em fə sē′mə) a disease of the lungs in which damage to the walls of the alveoli causes them to become permanently enlarged. This reduces the efficiency of the exchange of carbon dioxide and oxygen between blood and air.

en do crine glands (en′dō krin glandz) special organs in the body which produce hormones and release them into the bloodstream.

en do me tri um (en dō mē′trē əm) the soft tissue lining the uterus which varies in thickness during the menstrual cycle.

en do morph (en′dō môrf) a type of body build that has a heavy bone structure and pads of soft rounded flesh.

ep i did y mis (ep′ə did ə məs) small tubules in the male that lie on top and alongside the testes, used for storing sperm temporarily.

ep i dur al ca nal (ep′ə d(y)ur əl kə nal′) the lower part of the spinal column, where anaesthetic may be introduced to ease the pain of childbirth.

es tro gen (es′trə jən) one of the sex hormones produced by the ovaries that causes female characteristics in the body.

eth yl al co hol (eth′əl al′kə hol) the kind of alcohol that is contained in alcoholic drinks.

ex tent of train ing the amount of exercise necessary to improve one's fitness.

Fal lo pi an tubes (falō′pē ən tūbz) tubes in the female reproductive system connecting each of the two ovaries to the uterus.

fer men ta tion (fėr men tā′shən) the process by which yeast changes the sugar in plant substances to carbon dioxide and alcohol.

fe tus (fē′təs) the name for the developing baby as it grows in the uterus from the second month.

flex i bil i ty the ability to move your joints fully and easily.

fol li cle—stim ul at ing hor mone (FSH) (fol′əkəl stim′yu lāt ing hôr′mōn) a hormone produced by the pituitary gland which stimulates the production of sperm cells in the male and ova in the female.

genes (jēnz) parts of chromosomes which determine physical characteristics such as eye colour, hair texture, and height.

glu cose (glü′kōs) blood sugar, the most essential form of sugar for body energy.

gly co gen (glī′kə jən) a carbohydrate that is stored in the liver to be released as needed.

gon o coc cus germ (gon ə kak′əs jėrm) a bacteria that enters the body by way of the mucous membranes causing gonorrhea.

gon or rhe a (gon ə rē′ ə) the disease caused by the gonococcus bacteria. It is spread by sexual contact and if untreated spreads upward along the genital tract.

hang o ver a condition which occurs after drinking too much alcohol, characterized by headache, thirst, dizziness, and an upset stomach.

heart at tack the blockage of a coronary artery causing damage to part of the heart muscle.

heart rate the number of times the heart beats per minute.

her pes gen it al is (hėr′pēz jen ə tal′is) a virus disease passed by intimate skin contact that causes sores on the genitals.

hor mones (hôr′mōnz) substances released from the endocrine glands into the bloodstream which act on specific parts of the body.

hy per ten sion (hī pər ten′shən) abnormally high blood pressure. There are many causes.

hy po ther mi a (hī pə thėr′mē ə) a condition where the body temperature is reduced below normal, producing shivering, numbness, drowsiness, muscular weakness, apathy, and lack of appetite.

in ter val train ing a method of fitness training where a period of work is followed by a period of rest.

in tox i ca tion (in tok sə kā′shən) a condition of light-headedness occurring when alcohol has been absorbed into the blood stream.

i so met ric (ī sə met′rik) one of two basic types of exercise to develop muscular strength. In these exercises the muscle is contracted but does not move or change in length.

i so pro pyl al co hol (ī sə prō′pyl al′kə hol) rubbing alcohol, a poisonous alcohol that is used externally to reduce fever and cleanse wounds.

i so ton ic (ī sə ton′ic) one of two basic types of exercise to develop muscle strength. These are exercises in which muscles are contracted or lengthened while working against a load or force.

joint the area between two bones that allows the bones to move in relationship to one another.

kil o joule (kJ) (kil′ ə jül) a unit to measure energy produced by food and used in activity.

la bour the effort of giving birth to a child, involving three stages.

lac er a tion (las ər ā′shən) a deep cut in the flesh.

lac tic ac id (lak′tik as′id) a waste product of glycogen which is left in the muscles after exercise.

lig a ments (lig′ə mənts) strong fibrous bands that join one bone to another and keep the joint intact.

lymph sy stem (limf sis′təm) a network of small vessels (lymphatics) which drain fluid (lymph) from the body tissues. The lymphatics pass through the lymph nodes which filter out bacteria and drain into the venous system.

mar i jua na (mar ə wä′na) the drug obtained from the leaves and flowers of the hemp plant.

mei o sis (mī ō′sis) a process through which sperm cells and egg cells divide so that they contain only 23 chromosomes each.

men stru a tion (men strü ā′shən) the loss of the blood and soft tissue from the uterus.

me so morph (me′zō môrf) type of body build that has medium-heavy bones, little fat, and well developed muscles.

meth yl al co hol (meth′yl al′kə hol) a poisonous alcohol used in hair tonic and windshield washer fluid.

min er als (min′ər əlz) nonorganic elements which are essential for good health.

mo ru la (mȯ rə lə) a ball of many cells that develops into an embryo

move ment time the time it takes to activate the muscles.

mu cus (mū ′ kəs) a slimy substance secreted by the mucous membranes.

mus cle pull a condition when a muscle has been stretched beyond its capacity.

non—gon o coc cal u re thri tis (non gon ə kok əl yu rə thrī′təs) a widespread, sexually transmitted disease. It is thought to be caused by bacteria that can damage the reproductive organs of both males and females.

o va (ō′və) female egg cells.

o va ries (ō′və rēz) in the female reproductive system, the organs which produce ova.

o vu la tion (ō vü lā′shən) the release of an ovum by the ovaries.

ox y gen star va tion a condition when the muscles are not obtaining enough oxygen to convert glycogen to energy.

pen i cil lin (pen ə sil′ən) a drug produced from a mould which kills or inhibits the growth of bacteria.

phys i cal fit ness the ability of the entire body to function efficiently. It can be divided into two general areas: fitness related to the ability to perform certain physical skills, and fitness related to actual bodily health.

pi tu i tar y gland (pə tū′ə ter ē gland) a gland located on the underside of the brain that produces several hormones involving growth and sex characteristics.

pla cen ta (plə sen′tə) the organ which nourishes the fetus in the uterus.

plan tar warts (plan′tər warts) warts, usually found on the feet, that are caused by a virus.

pol y un sat u rat ed fat (pol′ī un sach ə rāt id fat) a type of unsaturated fat that is found in some nuts and seeds and does not contain cholesterol.

pow er the capacity to do strength activities quickly.

py lor ic valve (pī lôr′ik valv) a valve between the stomach and the small intestine.

pro ges ter one (prō jes′tər ōn) a female sex hormone secreted by the ovaries.

pros tate gland (prōs tāt gland) a gland in the male reproductive system that secretes a milky, alkaline substance that is a component of semen.

pro te ins (prō′tē inz) complex substances which, next to water, make up most of the body tissues. Proteins are contained in meat, fish, cheese, eggs, milk, grain, nuts, seeds, and legumes.

pu ber ty (pū′bər tē) a stage of development in humans when the reproductive system reaches maturity and becomes capable of reproduction.

pul mo nar y ar ter y (pul′mə ner ē är′tər ē) the artery that carries "used" blood from the heart to the lungs.

pul mo nar y cir cu la tion (pul′mə ner ē sėr kyu lā′shən) the movement of the blood from heart to lungs to heart.

pulse rate (puls rāt) the number of times the heart beats per minute as measured by the beat of the blood flow in the arteries.

re ac tion time the time it takes for the brain to perceive a stimulus, send a message to the muscles, and for the muscles to react.

res pi ra to ry sys tem (res′pə rə tô rē sis′təm) the body system involved with breathing.

Rh (Rhesus) fac tor a particular characteristic that is present in the blood of 85% of the population, and not in the other 15%.

sat u rat ed fat (sach′ə rāt ed fat) a fat from animal sources that contains cholesterol.

scro tum (skrō′təm) sack of skin that covers and protects the testes.

sed a tives (sed′ə tivs) substances which reduce activity and excitement.

se men (sē′mən) a mixture of fluids (fluid nutrient and a milky alkaline substance) and sperm that is ejaculated by the male.

sem i nal ves i cles (sem′ə nəl ves′ə kəlz) the organs in the male reproductive system that add a fluid nutrient to the sperm.

shin splint a swelling or inflammation of the sheath around the outside of the main bone of the lower leg, caused by continued jarring of the sheath.

shock acute failure of the circulation of blood to the body and to its extremities. Symptoms include decreased blood pressure, rapid pulse, pale clammy skin with slow breathing, and sometimes unconsciousness.

sil ver ni trate (sil′vər nī′trāt) an antiseptic used to treat the eyes of newborn babies to prevent infection from gonorrhea.

spe cif ic train ing certain kinds of exercises or activity undertaken to improve specific elements of physical fitness.

sperm the male sex cell produced by the testes.

sprain stretched or torn ligaments.

stam i na physical endurance.

ster oids (ster′oidz) a large group of compounds which include the sex hormones.

stroke a medical condition that occurs when the blood supply to the brain is stopped by a broken blood vessel or blood clot.

syph i lis (sif′ə lis) a serious bacterial disease spread by sexual contact which, if untreated, can cause severe damage to the body.

sys tem ic cir cu la tion (sis tem′ ik sėr kyu lā′ shən) the heart to body to heart movement of blood.

sys tol ic pres sure (sis tol′ik presh′ər) the higher of the two blood pressure readings. It measures the blood pressure at the moment the heart beats.

ten don i tis (ten dən ī′tis) a swelling or inflammation of the tendon.

tes tes (tes′tēz) the glands in the male that produce sperm cells.

tes tos ter one (tes tos′tər ōn) a male hormone secreted by the testes.

tet an us (tet′a nəs) a disease caused by the tetanus bacillus which enters the body through an open cut or sore. The disease causes spasm of the muscles, particularly the jaw muscles—hence the name lockjaw.

thy ro tro pin (thī rə trō′pən) a hormone produced by the pituitary gland that stimulates the thyroid gland to produce thyroxin.

thy rox in (thı rock′ sən) a hormone secreted by the thyroid gland, that regulates the rate at which cells use up food.

tra che a (trā′kē ə) the windpipe, the part of the respiratory system which extends from the larynx to the bronchi.

train ing ef fect the effect of pushing the lungs and heart beyond their normal capacity by exercise so that they begin to adapt to doing greater work.

tran quil liz ers (trang′kwəl īz ərz) drugs reducing anxiety.

trich o mo ni a sis (trik ə mō′nī ə səs) an easily treated form of vaginitis caused by a tiny one-celled organism.

um bil i cal cord (um bil′ə kəl kôrd) a tube connecting the embryo to the placenta through which blood vessels carry nutrients and wastes to and from the embryo.

un sat u rated fat (un sach′ə rā tid fat) a fat which does not contain cholesterol, found in vegetables such as corn and peanuts.

u re thra (ū rē′thrə) the tube which carries urine from the bladder out of the body. In males it also carries semen.

u ter us (ū′tər əs) the organ in female mammals that holds the developing fetus.

va gi na (və jī′ nə) the birth canal in the female reproductive system, a strong, elastic passage that connects the cervix to the outside genitals.

vag in al thrush (vaj′ə nəl thrush) a vaginal fungus which can affect females. It is not necessarily linked to sexual contact but can be passed that way.

vas de fer ens (vas de′fər enz) tubes that store and carry sperm from the testes to the prostate gland in the male.

veg e tar i an di et (vej ə tār′ē ən di ət) a diet containing only plant foods. If the diet contains dairy products and eggs it is called lacto-ovo-vegetarian.

vein (vān) a thin-walled blood vessel that carries blood to the heart from different parts of the body.

ven tri cle (ven′trə kəl) one of the two lower chambers of the heart.

ven ules (ven′ûlz) tiny vessels that, along with capillaries, form a mesh between arteries and veins.

vi rus (vī′rəs) one of a group of simple micro-organisms, smaller than bacteria, which reproduce in a living host cell causing disease.

vi ta mins (vī′tə minz) a group of unrelated substances that must be present in the diet in order to maintain good health. The body cannot make these substances.

warm-up a period before any strenuous activity in which the muscles to be used are stretched and loosened to prepare them for work.

weight train ing a program of isotonic exercises, using weights as the load, to increase the amount of work the muscles can do.

wet dream a build-up of sperm and fluid (semen) which is released during sleep.

zy gote (zī′gōt) a fertilized ovum.

INDEX

ACKNOWLEDGEMENTS

PHOTOGRAPHS

Page 14, Tourism British Columbia; Pages 18, 19, 20, 25, 26, 27, 28, 29, 30, 46, 62, 63, Peter Paterson; Page 38, National Film Board, Phototeque, Murray MacGowan; Page 43, Josh Goldhar, Town of Mississauga Aquatic Club; Page 51, Terence Kavanagh M.D., from *The Healthy Heart Program* by Terence Kavanagh M.D., Van Nostrand Reinhold Ltd., Toronto, 1980; Page 55, Bicycles: courtesy: DiSalle Bicycle Co., Harry Bleyenberg, Photographer, Toronto; Page 58, Birgitte Nielsen, Page 64, Jon Easton, Photographer; Pages 67, 71, The Globe and Mail, Toronto; Page 80, Ontario Ministry of Industry and Tourism; Page 95, Photograph from Miller Services, Toronto, Ontario; Page 108, The Metropolitan Toronto and Region Conservation Authority; Page 112, From *A Child is Born* by Lennart Nilsson. English Translation Copyright © 1966, 1977 by Dell Publishing Co., Inc. Originally published in Swedish under the title *Ett Barn Blir Till* by Albert Bonniers Forlag. Copyright © 1965 by Albert Bonniers Forlag, Stockholm. Revised edition Copyright © 1976 by Lennart Nilsson, Mirjam Furuhjelm, Alex Ingelman-Sundberg, Cales Wirson. Used by permission of Delacorte Press /Seymour Lawrence; Page 126, Miller Services; Pages 127 and 130, Harry Bleyenberg, Photographer, Toronto; Page 132, Birgitte Nielsen; Page 139, Miller Services; Page 145, (left) Women's Bureau, Ontario Ministry of Labour, (right) Ministry of Education, Experience '77, and Women's Studies, Toronto Board of Education; Page 146, (left) The Globe and Mail, Toronto, (right) Women's Bureau, Ontario Ministry of Labour; Page 154, Photo courtesy of Ontario Ministry of Industry and Tourism; Page 157, Planned Parenthood of Toronto.

CHARTS

Page 34, *The Sportsmedicine Book* by Gabe Mirkin, M.D. and Marshall Hoffman, published by Little, Brown and Company, Boston, 1978. Originally published by the President's Council on Physical Fitness and Sports. Page 46, The pictures and instructions for "The Step Test" are based on materials from *Fitness For Life* by Charles B. Corbin and Ruth Lindsey, published by Scott, Foresman and Company, Glenview, Illinois, 1979, and are reprinted here by permission of Fred W. Kasch, Ph.D. Page 47, From *Fitness For Life* by Charles B. Corbin and Ruth Lindsey. Copyright © 1979 by Scott, Foresman and Company. Reprinted by permission. Page 49, Rosseau Publishing Corporation Ltd. 791 St. Clair Ave. W., Toronto. To obtain a complete Testing Program, write: Fit Kit, Box 5100, Thornhill, Ontario, Canada, L3T 4S5. Pages 72, 85, 88, 89, From *Nutrition and Physical Fitness* by Bogart, Briggs, and Kellaway, published by W.B. Saunders Co. Canada Ltd., Toronto, 1966. Page 86, source: Alan Robertson. Pages 91, 92, 93, "A Guide to Better Nutrition", H.J. Heinz Co. of Canada, 250 Bloor St. E., Toronto.

ILLUSTRATIONS
Colin A. Gillies: Pages 16, 31, 32, 35, 36, 37, 40, 50, 57, 60, 78, 79, 87, 94, 97, 98, 99, 105, 106, 123, 133, 143, 151. Peter Grau: Pages 22, 23, 33, 49, 52, 68, 70, 73, 74, 75, 83, 84, 90, 103, 109, 128-129, 148, 150, 165. Robin Hamilton: Pages 42, 45, 69, 76, 104, 134, 137, 159, 161. Dorothy Irwin: Pages 114, 115, 116, 117, 121, 124.

The CSA symbol is reprinted here by permission of the Canadian Standards Association, 178 Rexdale Boulevard, Rexdale, Ontario, M9W 1R3.

The metric usage in this text has been reviewed by the Metric Screening Office of the Canadian General Standards Board.

Metric Commission Canada has granted use of the National Symbol for Metric Conversion.